FRANCE.

LIST OF TREATIES, &c.

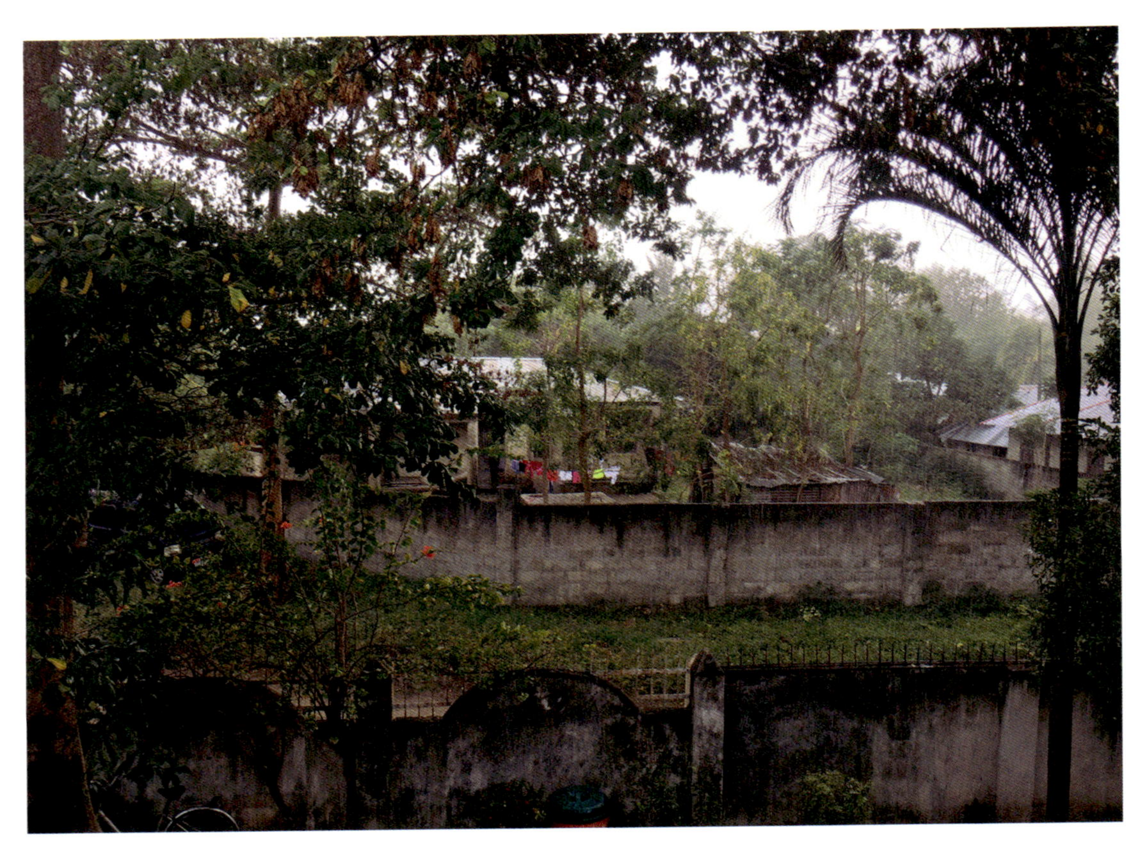

Zarina Bhimji
Lead White

HENI 

YARROW'S SHALLOW DRAFT STEAMERS.

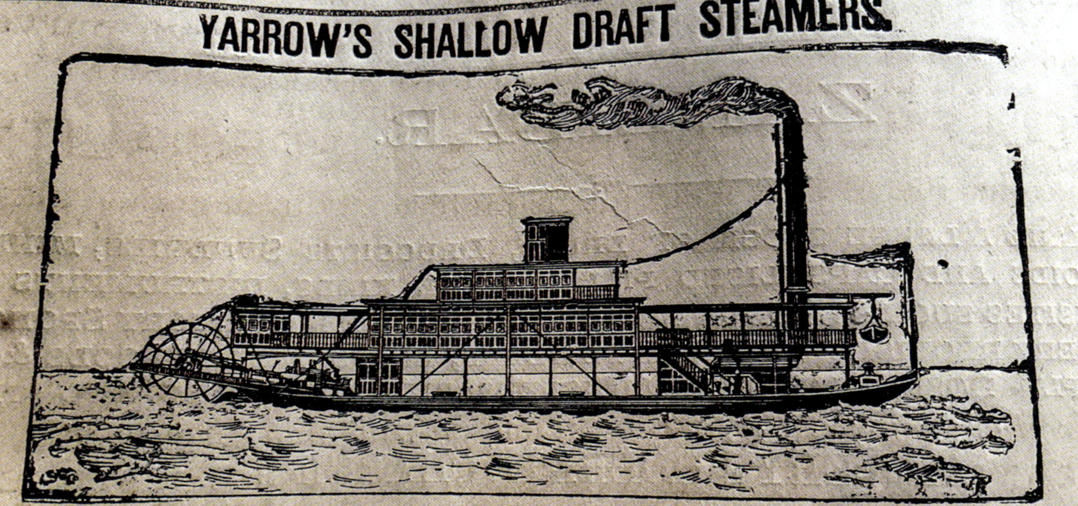

STERNWHEEL STEAMERS have been found by experience to be the best type of vessel for shallow river navigation, and of these Messrs. YARROW have constructed a large number of successful examples for all parts of the world. Vessels on this system are constructed when required, to draw as little as 6 inches.

Messrs. YARROW lately built the sternwheelers "Mosquito" and "Herald" for the British Government, for service on the Zambesi.

They were constructed in floatable sections (capable of shipment), which were simply bolted together, avoiding thereby the costly and difficult process of riveting up and launching.

For full particulars apply to—

CONTENTS

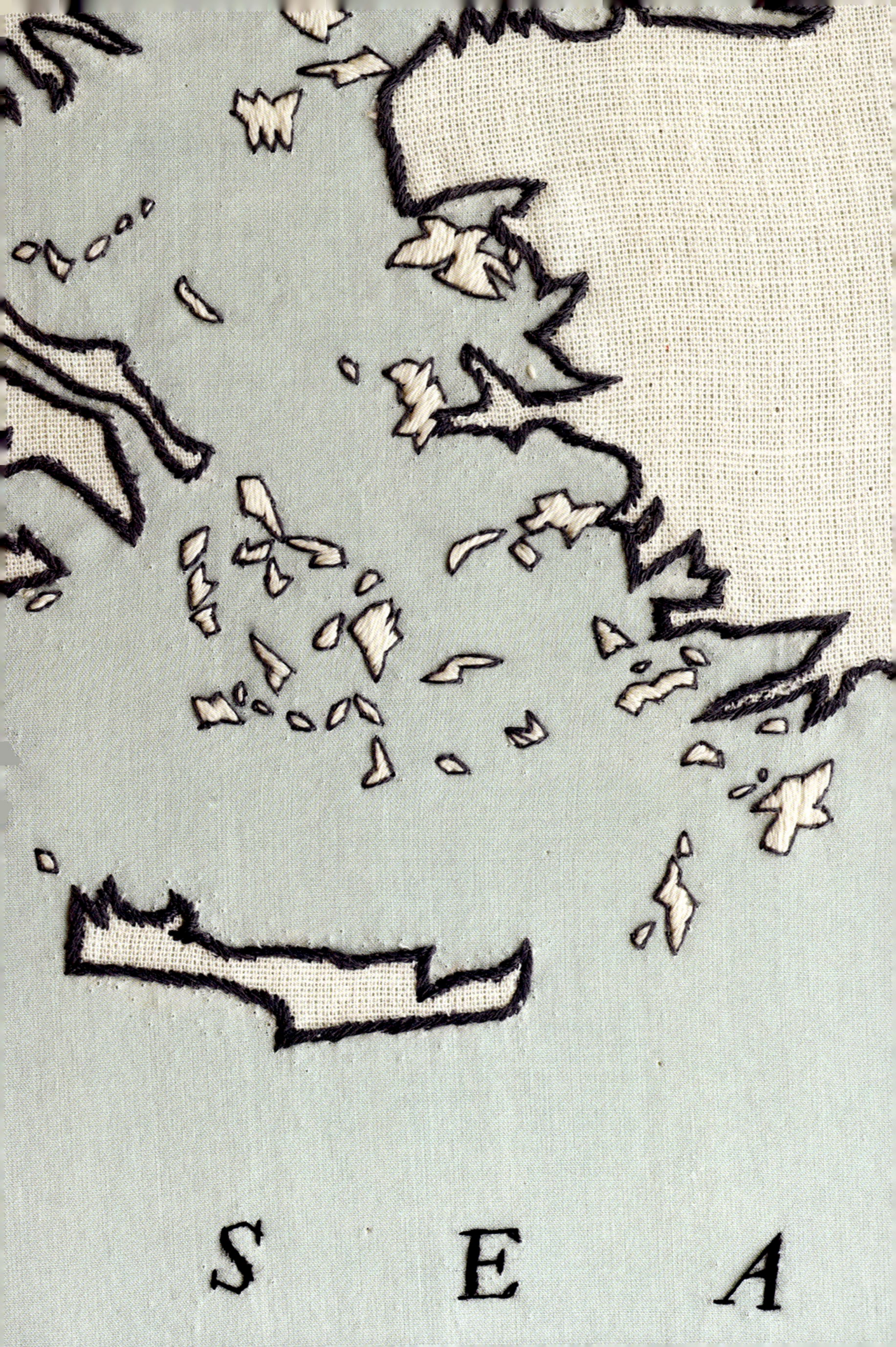

S E A

PERIPHERAL VISION: ZARINA BHIMJI'S *LEAD WHITE*
Ann Gallagher

There is an inherent tension in Zarina Bhimji's work, between what has become its underlying subject – the complex postcolonial narrative that links East Africa, South Asia and the United Kingdom – and the strikingly oblique way in which it is addressed formally and conceptually in her films, photographs and installations. Although infused with references to human presence, Bhimji's work achieves its resonance through its intense focus on landscapes and architectural spaces, and on the abstract or poetic qualities of details. She devotes a painterly attention to the effects of light, texture and colour, and to communicating atmosphere and sensory perceptions: 'Light is a key element in my composition and becomes just as intricate and important as human presence or the lack thereof. The stillness creates a suspension of everyday life, and yet there is a narrative inferred by way of mood and a sense of mystery and incompleteness.'[1]

This sense of mystery is enhanced by the almost forensic scrutiny of Bhimji's gaze, and in the camera's lingering focus in her films, as if in search of evidence to seek understanding. Research has long underpinned and preceded the artist's production, undertaken in libraries and archives, as well as on location trips. Multiple perspectives are accumulated and absorbed, and yet overt explanation or assertion is entirely absent in the works that culminate. These function rather as poignant studies allowing space and time for reflection on the painful histories that contribute to the realities of the present day. While Bhimji's 2018 installation of photographs and maps, *Lead White*, can be seen as a new direction for her work, with its use of digital photography and embroidery, in many ways it is a distillation of both the methods she has developed and the perspectives she has accumulated over the past two decades.

> 'During my first visit back to Uganda in 1998, I listened to the land, to the sounds in the air, to the smell of guns.'[2]

Bhimji's family came separately as refugees to Britain in 1974, having been forced into hiding and then to flee Uganda following Idi Amin's 1972 decree to expel around 80,000 people of South Asian descent. Eight years later Bhimji began studying art at Leicester Polytechnic, and went on to attend Goldsmiths' College (1983–86) and the Slade School of Art (1987–89) in London. The work she was producing by the 1990s combined language, memory and objects that linked her Indian heritage, East African childhood and experience of living in a Western culture. At the age of 35 she made the first of many visits to Uganda, prompted by a growing interest in the way in which the events of 1972–74 were documented and discussed, and the implications for individuals who had been affected by them. Among these were the legal and bureaucratic issues Ugandan Asians were encountering over documentation lost during the expulsion, decades before the recent Windrush scandal, when it emerged that British subjects were being denied their basic rights of citizenship. This initial trip to Uganda marked the beginning of a new method of working for the artist, involving background research conducted on location and the discovery of a particular affinity to the medium of film. As well as a series of photographs titled *Love*, 1998–2007, her first major film installation resulted from these visits back to Uganda, *Out of Blue*, 2002, commissioned by Documenta 11. *Out of Blue* is an extraordinarily moving portrait of the land of Bhimji's birth, in which the element of allegory in her previous work finds its essence. Writing of the film in 2003, the late Stuart Hall observed that, 'The eerily evacuated Ugandan landscapes ... speak volumes through absence, summoning up the profound sense of emptiness and loss which forced exile produces, and the silent devastation left behind by those who wreak a brutal revenge on difference.'[3]

Narrative is built up through the motion of the camera over the landscape and empty buildings, punctuated by sparse action, such as the appearance of smoke, and sounds including gunshots and voices. Key to providing rhythm and texture, the soundtrack in Bhimji's films is a component that is researched and recorded alongside the mute imagery, but is added only after filming is complete. The sounds in *Out of Blue* offer suggestions of atmosphere or narrative, in the same way that on occasion an image provides a pointer or clue that contributes to meaning. A sign on an airport building positions the location of the film, but collective memory is relied upon to add the specifics of the exodus of Ugandan Asians from Entebbe Airport. Echoes of different waves of migration in more recent history contribute to the effect of evoking universal rather than personal experience. The sound of mosquitoes – recorded by the artist at the London School of Hygiene and Tropical Medicine – is a recurring motif in *Out of Blue*, and the voice of the Sufi singer, composer and musician, Abida Parveen, has a strong presence. While making the film, Bhimji listened to Parveen's singing repeatedly. Both the sound of the ghazals[4] and the poetry of the Urdu lyrics enabled her to 'enter into a space that contained me with her words and sounds' and 'became like a thread that I was able to unwind to develop a structure for the film.'[5]

Bhimji's use of film has allowed her to explore to the fullest its potential to communicate the diverse sensations evoked by a particular setting. She describes working on location with a camera as being in a laboratory, where she can test out ideas through seeing, hearing, touching, smelling and feeling. In conversation, the artist frequently interconnects sensory perception – she talks of 'drinking in details', 'listening to a room' and 'tactile, moist light.' Spending time in physical proximity to the subject matter of her project also allows for contingencies to occur, for the unexpected to emerge as prospective material or for chance conversations to lead to new sources of information. Sound is researched as meticulously as imagery for Bhimji's films, and chance also plays a role in its selection. An encounter with an MRI scanner during a period of illness, for example, provided the cacophony of dramatic noises which were integrated into the soundtrack of her film *Jangbar* 2015:

> My project is about learning to listen to difference … Listening with the eyes, listening to changes in tone, difference of colour. It attempts to link to similar disturbances that have taken place in Kosovo and Rwanda. The work … is about making sense through the medium of aesthetics. It is a question that is close to my heart since the significant ethical issues have a resonance for me. I want to register these issues, to mark what has happened; elimination, extermination and erasure. Within the broader question of difference, an important part of the project would be the possibility of creative difference. Such a combination of personal and public aspects holds a particular resonance at the start of the twenty-first century … I would hope that the work that emerges would be distanced from its personal or historical specifications.[6]

Beginning with her research into the events in Uganda in the early 1970s, Bhimji's interest has gradually broadened to encompass the circumstances of its prehistory, including the division of Africa by European powers following the Berlin Conference of 1884–85 and the subsequent occupation and colonisation of the continent. Her research has led her to visit port towns in Western India and farms and factories in Kenya, to examine records and maps in archives in Edinburgh, London, Mumbai and Zanzibar. She withholds drawing conclusions from the evidence she accumulates in the resulting works, but allows imagery encountered in the present day to delicately act as an echo of past events or as 'symptoms of strange links between history, memory and fantasy.'[7]

Three films, originally conceived as one, cover different aspects of this research. *Waiting*, 2009, focusses on the production of sisal[8] – a key export, which had been dependent on slave labour in East Africa, until it was gradually taken over by South Asian immigrants – in textile factories in Kenya. Bhimji has described sisal as a metaphor for hair in this film, the hair of Europeans being tended by the workers. *Yellow Patch*, 2011, meanwhile, was filmed on location in Gujarat, where many Indians, including Bhimji's parents, migrated to East Africa from its ports. Immigration is thought to have begun in the search for economic opportunity, but during the British colonial period many thousands of Indians journeyed first to Zanzibar, then on to Kenya and Uganda, to work on the empire project in clerical positions or as traders. Among those who remained were workers recruited to construct the Ugandan railway, begun in 1896, which was to link Mombasa to Kisumu on the shores of Lake Victoria, along the old East African slave route. Abandoned railway stations on this line feature in the third film, *Jangbar*, with signage showing the three clearly delineated classes of travel that operated on the trains. Left unsaid, or merely implied, is the information about the many lives that were lost in the construction of what was known back in Britain as 'the Lunatic Line'.

The name Zanzibar is derived from Arabic, meaning 'land' or 'coast of blacks'. *Jangbar* is the Gujarati name for Zanzibar. The region's history differs from mainland East Africa due to its strategic position as a trading post on the Indian Ocean, and its historic links with Persia and Arabia, as evidenced by words that infiltrated the Zanzibar dialect of Swahili. The Portuguese were the first European power to gain control of Zanzibar, and held it as a tributary for almost 200 years, until it came under the domination of the Sultan of Oman in the early seventeenth century, and gradually became established as a centre for both the spice and slave trades. The growing influence of the British Empire was formalised when Zanzibar was claimed as a protectorate in 1890, although the Sultans remained as nominal rulers until independence in 1963. The Sultan of Zanzibar is even said to have had his Austin Princess limousine drive the young British Princess Margaret around the main island in 1956. Zanzibar City had become an important colonial hub, as well as a base for expeditions into the heart of Africa (David Livingstone set out from there on his last expedition in 1866, and his physician John Kirk became British Consul in the city). Despite being the target of multiple invasions and occupations for centuries until gaining independence in 1963, and joining with Tanganyika as the new country Tanzania in 1964, Zanzibar maintained its importance in the region as a centre of commerce and opportunity. For South Asians living in the region around the time of Bhimji's birth it signified a place of progress, of possibility, and of hope in a growing equality.

Much of the source material that prompted Bhimji's installation *Lead White* was accumulated in the same way as the storyboards she compiles for her films, through observing details and researching information, a large amount of which – in this case – was found in the National Archives in Zanzibar. Bhimji describes this research activity as being akin to the work of a detective or investigator. The evidence she seeks is in the traces of real lives, of people's actions and motivations, the micro-details that contribute to an unfathomably complex and morally ambiguous history. While human presence is mostly absent from Bhimji's work, it is always implied: it is the perspective of individuals that she strives to imagine, and which lies at the heart of her work.

The variously sized, large-scale photographs assembled together in *Lead White* echo the steady focus on details in Bhimji's films. Her interest is in the framing of these details, highlighting both the realities of society and the vulnerability of individual lives, which resonate beyond a specific historical narrative, becoming 'meditations on legality, power and beauty. I would like to tell a history which is not adequately discussed, by bringing a fresh perspective to things. By putting things together, visually a new meaning can arise.'[9] The focus of Bhimji's lens – which enables the artist, and the viewer, to examine each subject on a microscopic level – encompasses gestures in handwritten letters in coloured ink, the lines and texture of paper, the design of official stamps and seals on documents produced by named or anonymous officials and clerks, and traces of paper clips and white cotton ribbons attaching pages together. The 'Lead White' of the title is taken from the name of a lead carbonate used as a painting medium across cultures since at least the pre-Christian period, and the principal white pigment used in classical European oil painting. It was gradually replaced in the nineteenth century by zinc and titanium white, as knowledge of its toxicity became better known. For Bhimji, this 'old white' is the colour she retained as an impression from her archive examinations, and like her film titles *Out of Blue* and *Yellow Patch*, express both an overall mood and a linguistic association.[10]

Words in the stamps, letters and documents are often clearly legible, and although highly resonant as pieces of factual information, are positioned delicately in the composition of photographs as if they are archaeological vestiges. 'The General Act of the Conference of Berlin' can be discerned as a heading on a document signed on February 26, 1885, while another is titled 'Congo Free State', under which is the beginning of a list of treaties with foreign powers. Embossed stamps from various departments of the 'Government of India' appear repeatedly, as well as from other colonial territories and from European consulates in Zanzibar. There is a section of a typed letter from the 'President of The English Club', an establishment exclusively for British expatriate and Royal Navy members. There are appearances of the black stamp of the British and Foreign Anti-Slavery Society, with the motto 'Am I Not a Man and a Brother'; as well as a heading 'Book of Free Slaves'; while an extract from a letter contains the sentence 'The Colonial Office is sorely puzzled to know what to do with the slaves rescued by our cruisers on the east coast of Africa'. Ominously, several photographs contain the words 'Secret Department', and one includes the heading 'Secret No 15'.

Details of collections of postage stamps from across multiple territories speak of peoples linked by the distant European powers that ruled their lands, but what predominates are the colours and designs: palm trees and flowers; Llandovery Falls in Jamaica; or the Sultan of Zanzibar juxtaposed with an image of cloves, the principal symbol of commerce and wealth in the region. The image of Britannia crops up in a stamp from Trinidad; Queen Victoria appears on one from Canada; while a picture of a steam ship and the words *'Etat Independent de Congo'* proclaims itself triumphantly on another. These minute vestiges of visual culture function as banal yet powerful reminders of territorial dominance.

Lead White shares the power of intense focus found in Bhimji's film work, with its nuanced imagery and sound, but with what she describes as containing 'implied sound' resonating from the visual imagery found in the archives from which she gathered her source material. If the groups of photographs in *Lead White* have a precedent in the composition of Bhimji's films, the embroidered works that form part of the installation also have a precursor in her work. *Untitled (A Sketch)*, 1999, includes three dresses made out of maps of the United Kingdom, East Africa and India, functioning as metaphors for the three realms of influence on the artist. The maps of territory in *Lead White* are more specifically indicative of political history, although maps designating colonial territories by colour are remembered by a decreasing age demographic globally. Once again, issues are abstracted and held at one remove, with considerable attention devoted to the aesthetic qualities of each object. Alongside the high resolution digital photographs, the use of embroidery – a traditional craft technique used in multiple cultures – allows the work to reflect its tension between present and past, and enhances the relationship between the specific and the universal.

Bhimji specifies that her film works are experienced as large room projections, encouraging a full experience of all the physical sensations they evoke. *Lead White* is similarly conceived as an immersive environment. The poetry of the visual compositions in the photographs and the beauty of the embroidered maps, through enhanced colouring and texture, make evident that Bhimji uses form and perspective not to mirror her subject, but cumulatively to bring it into sharper relief. The sheer matter-of-fact nature of the material may seem at odds with its presentation, and yet viewing through the lens of the artist's vision provides its strength. We are reminded that humanity can perhaps best be questioned and sought to be understood through the peripheral vision that Bhimji is so eloquent in communicating, and which evokes in us a response that is all the more powerful.

1
Borchardt-Hume, Achim and Bühler, Kathleen, 'From Politics to Poetry' in *Zarina Bhimji*, (Whitechapel Gallery/ Kunstmuseum Bern/The New Art Gallery Walsall/ Ridinghouse, 2012), p. 35.

2
Lores, Maite, 'Out of Blue', *Contemporary Art*, issue 49 (2003), p. 60.

3
Hall, Stuart, 'Maps of Emergency: Fault Lines and Tectonic Plates' in Gilane Tawadros and Sarah Campbell, eds., *Fault Lines: Contemporary African Art and Shifting Landscapes*, (London: Iniva, 2003), p. 33.

4
A *ghazal* is a rhyming poem that origantes from Arabic verse, usually on the subject of romantic loss.

5
From a conversation between Ann Gallagher and Zarina Bhimji, March 2018.

6
From the film treatment for Zarina Bhimji's *Out of Blue*.

7
Demos, TJ, 'Zarina Bhimji: Cinema of Affect' in *Zarina Bhimji*, (Whitechapel Gallery/Kunstmuseum Bern/The New Art Gallery Walsall/Ridinghouse, 2012), p. 20.

8
Sisal is a strong fibre commonly used in ropes and rugs.

9
From a conversation between Ann Gallagher and Zarina Bhimji, March 2018.

10
Out of Blue was originally the subtitle 'out of the blue' of the film. *Yellow Patch* is a remembered expression used by Doris Lessing in a lecture.

SURCHARGE INVERTED

This place has a view of the tower, palace and harem. It's Friday morning and an inspection of the troops is under way. Inside the camera is a panorama of the city from a roof in Shangani. The many ships anchored in the harbour show the large volume of trade passing through the port. The walk to the museum was short although it felt long because of the humidity. Wherever Fatima travelled she bought postcards. They were black and white. One was of three women and the other showed the destruction inside the Beit al-Ajaib after the bombardment of 1896. Fatima found the postcards had a voice and she heard the voice saying, 'You have destroyed me. I was once beautiful architecture.' This is how it all began. Whilst on her research trip Fatima met Professor Karim Bhaloo. He was introduced to her as a professor of history, an advisor and principal curator at the city's museums. He spent a lot of time with her discussing many aspects of the food, music, family relationships and history, and he spoke about the archives. Fatima was developing a script for a film.

The landscape had a lush beauty thanks to the rain, with sunshine, a dramatic sky and fertile land. Fatima was looking aimlessly through the archives when she noticed a tall, slim, elegant man working at a desk. He reminded her of colonial India and Africa. The postcards spoke to her again; they seemed to be on her side, allowing her to feel close to her instincts.

Fatima had taken many trips to the Indian Ocean and felt very close to its eastern shore. There is something about the way the Indian Ocean pounds. She would often lie on the deep verandas, listening to the sounds of the sea. They create a space in her head; there is so much to think about. The dhows that travelled from Kutch... Fatima's mother was dying. As she looked out at the Indian Ocean she cried. She could not stop crying. She remembered hearing how her mother's uncle lived in Mombasa. They were the wealthy side of the family. He lost a finger in a factory accident. Fatima thought, 'I don't know what happened and now I cannot ask her.'

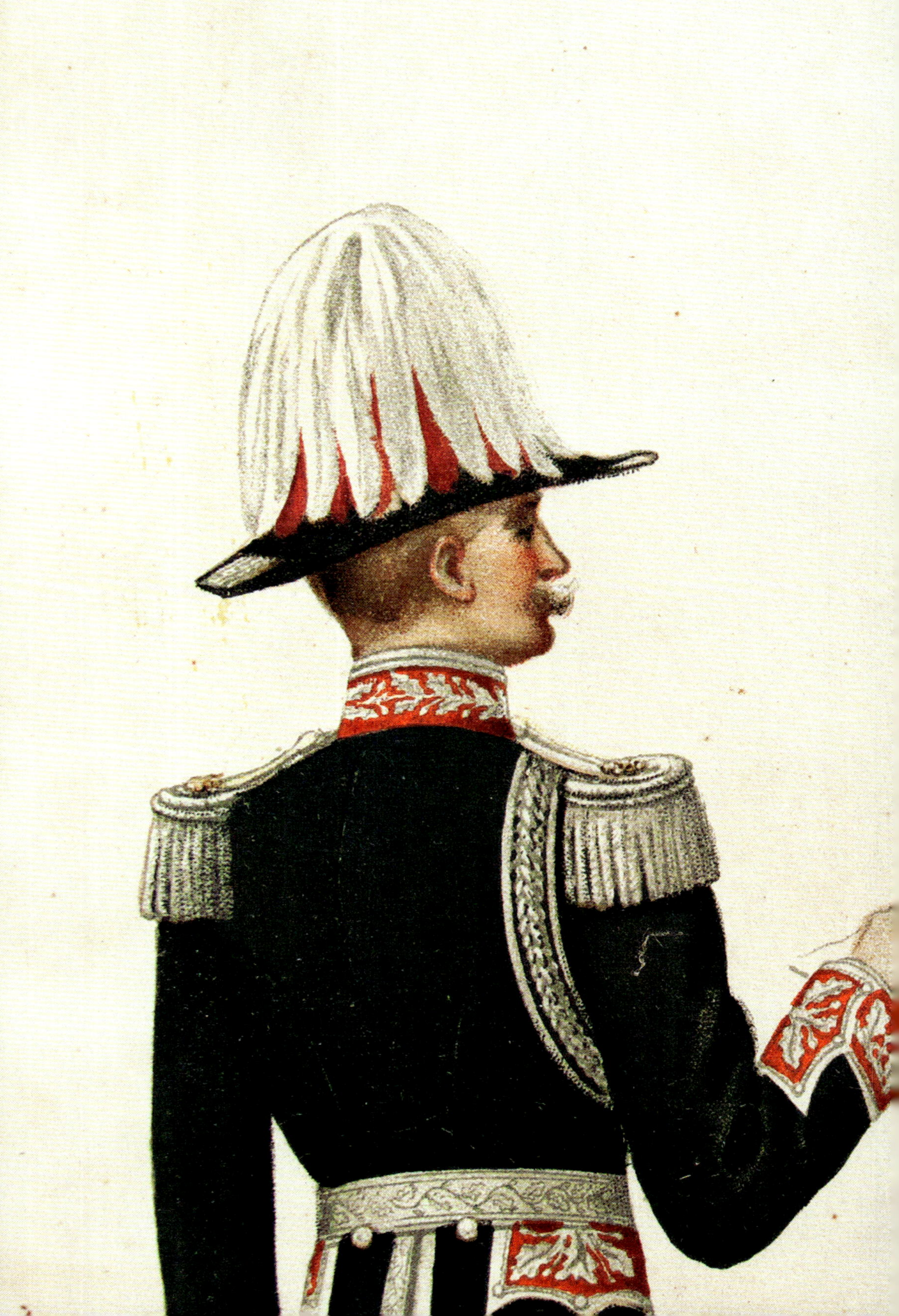

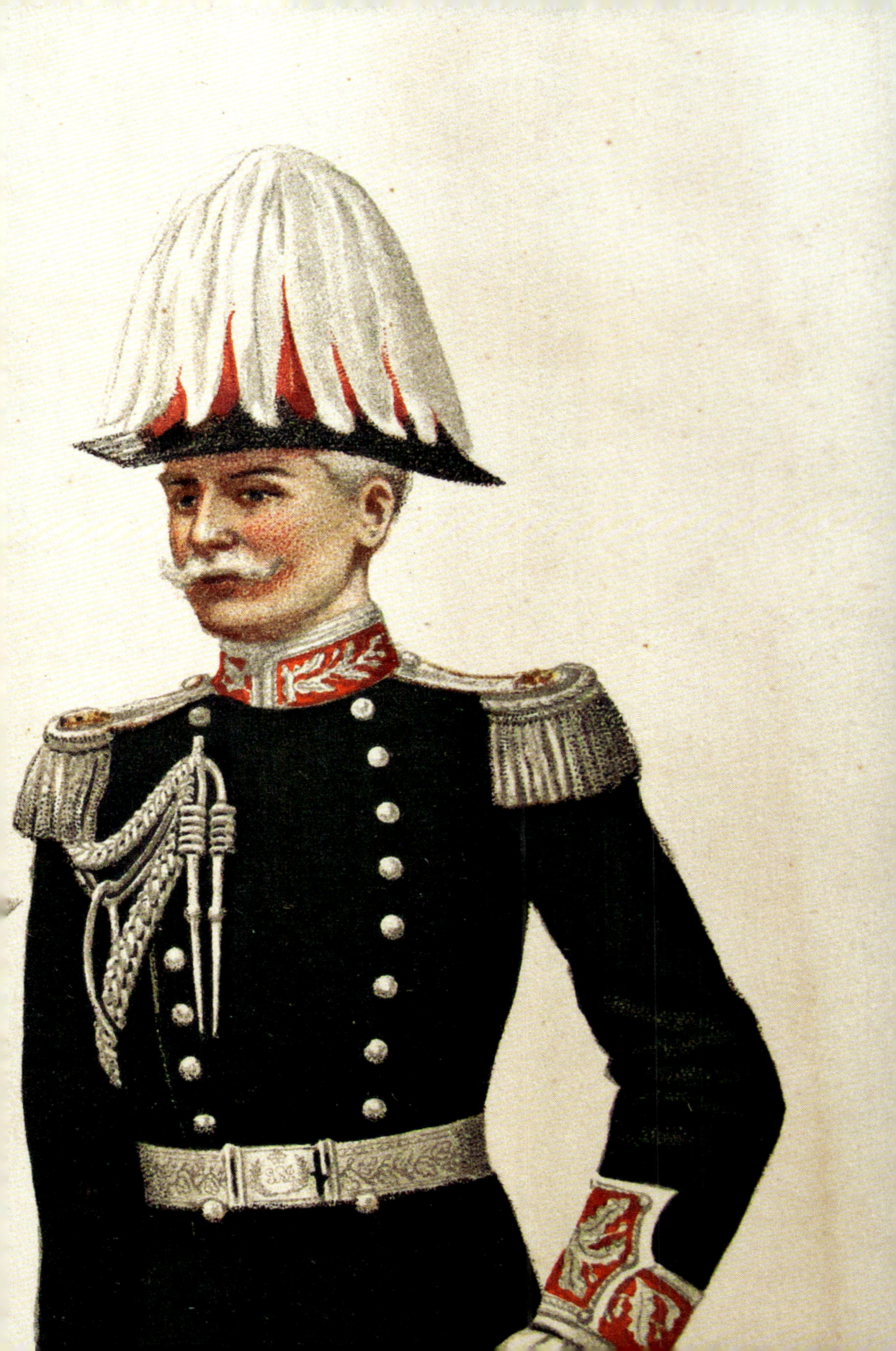

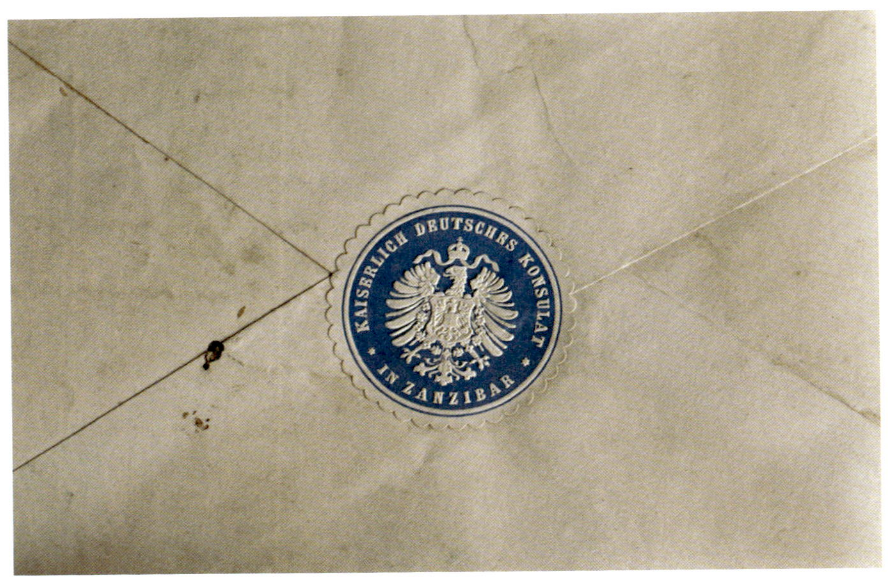

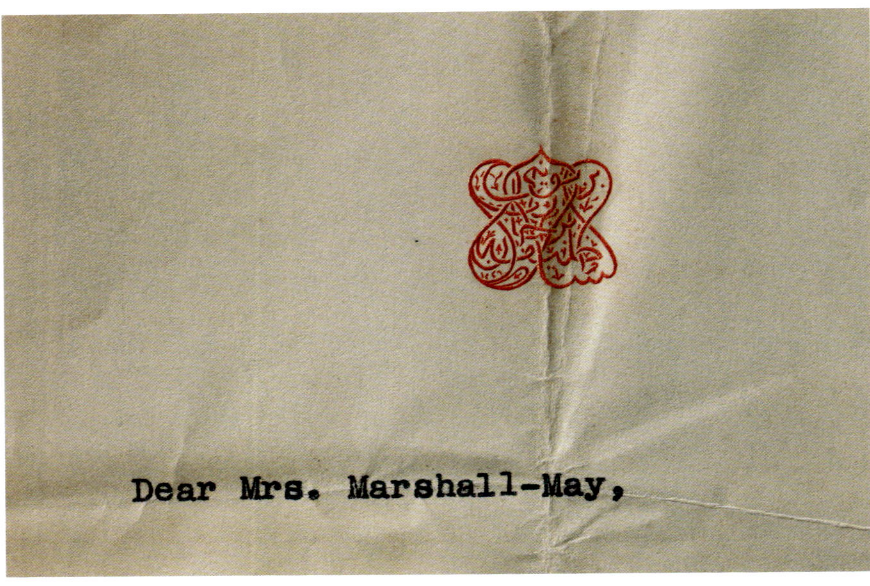
Dear Mrs. Marshall-May,

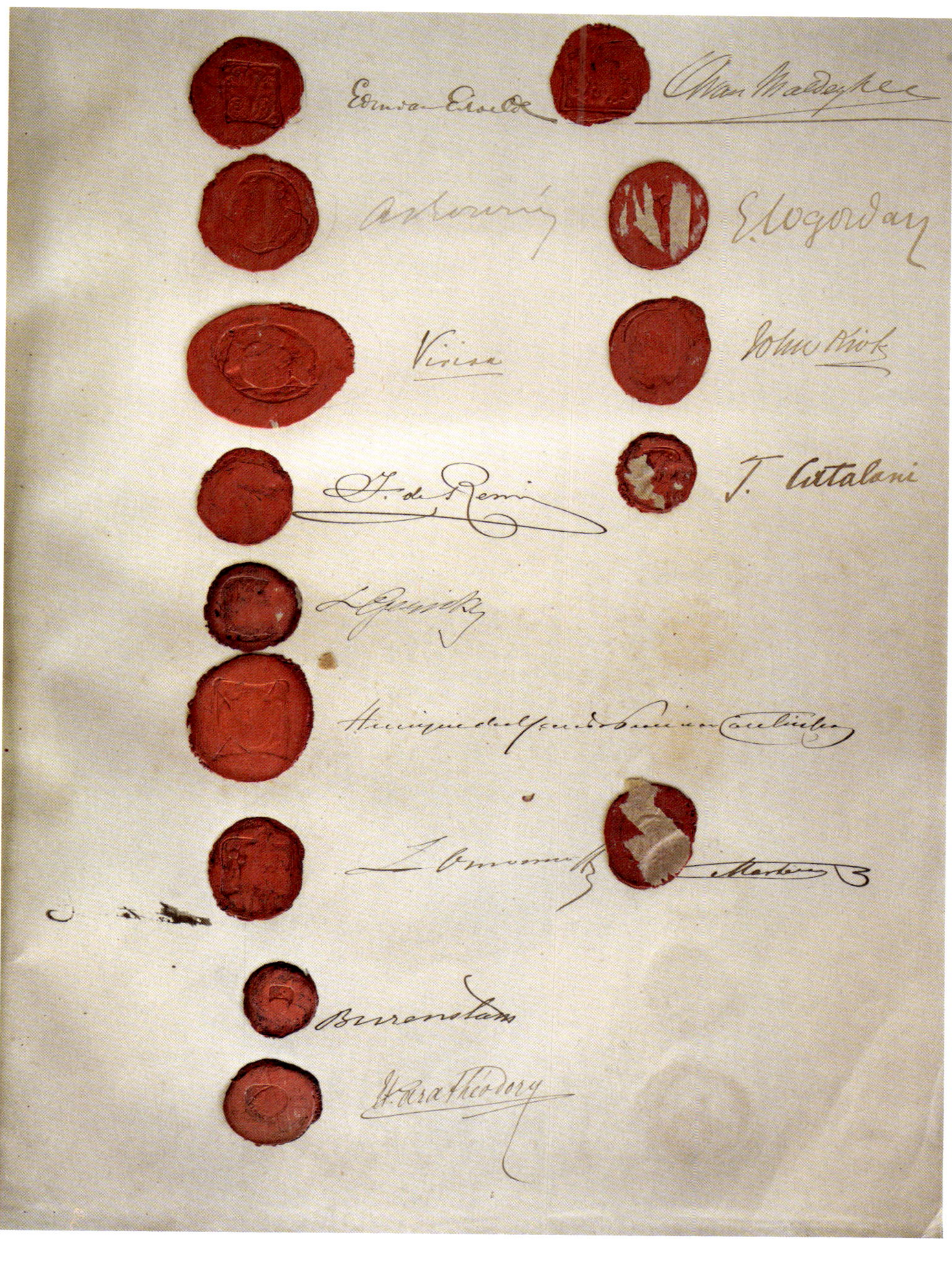

RESIDENT · ZANZIBAR

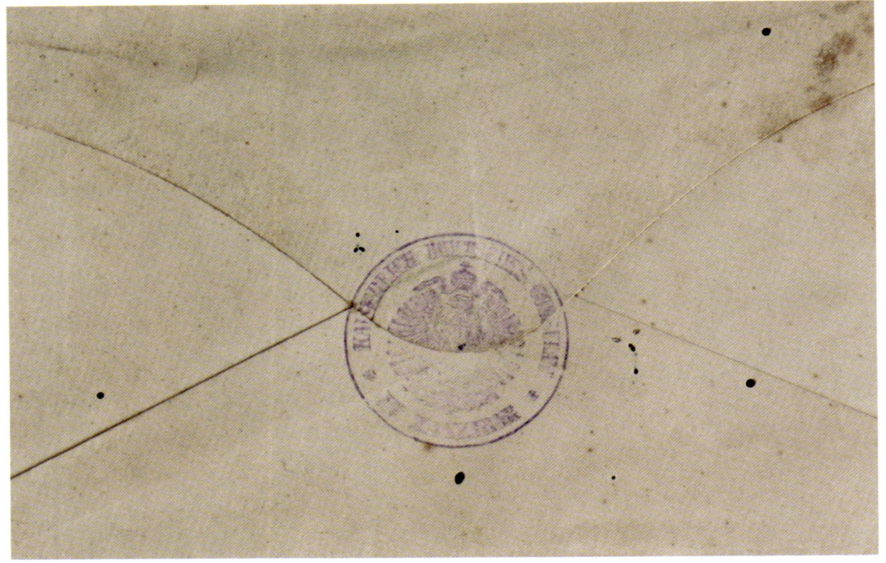

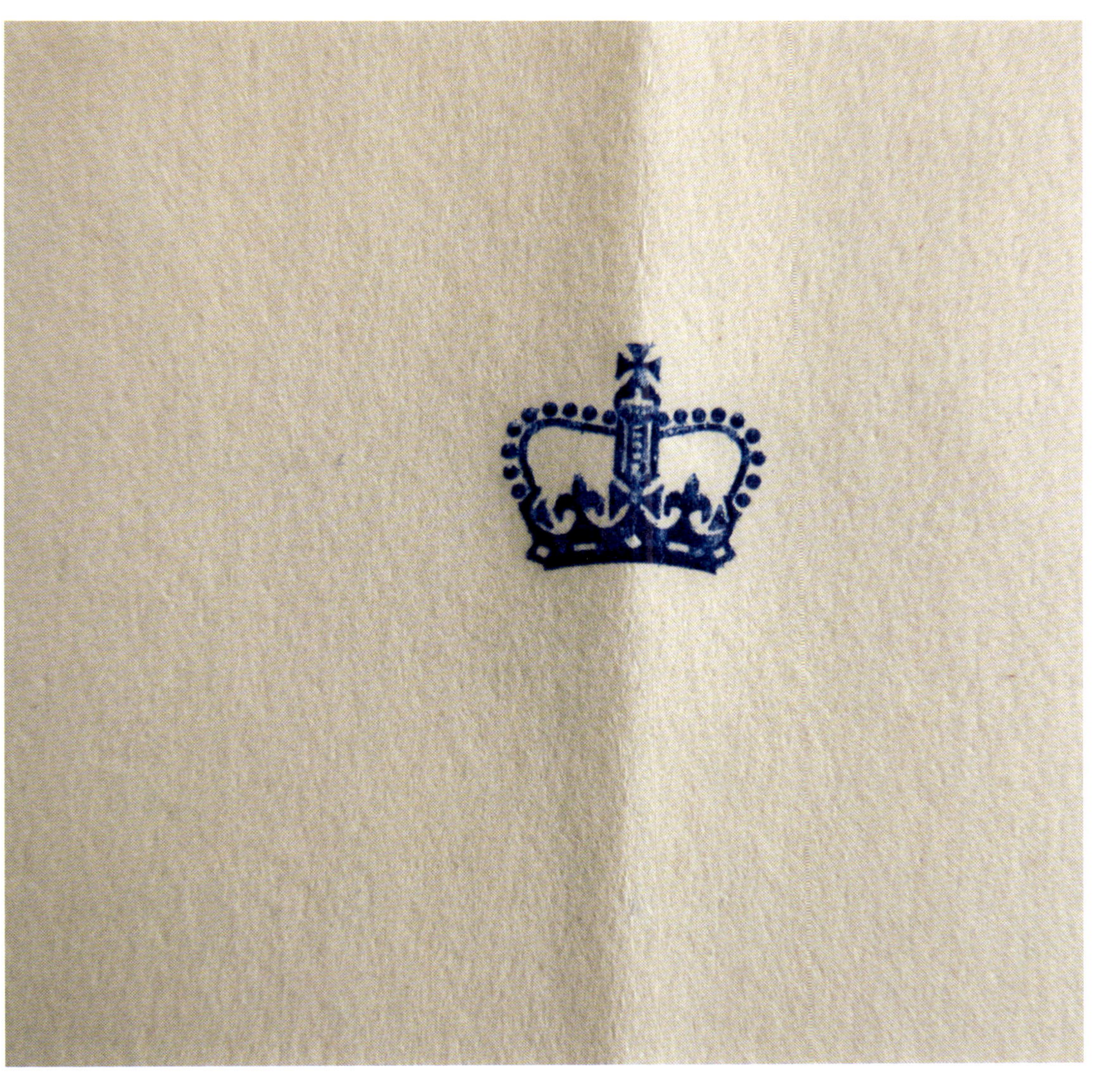

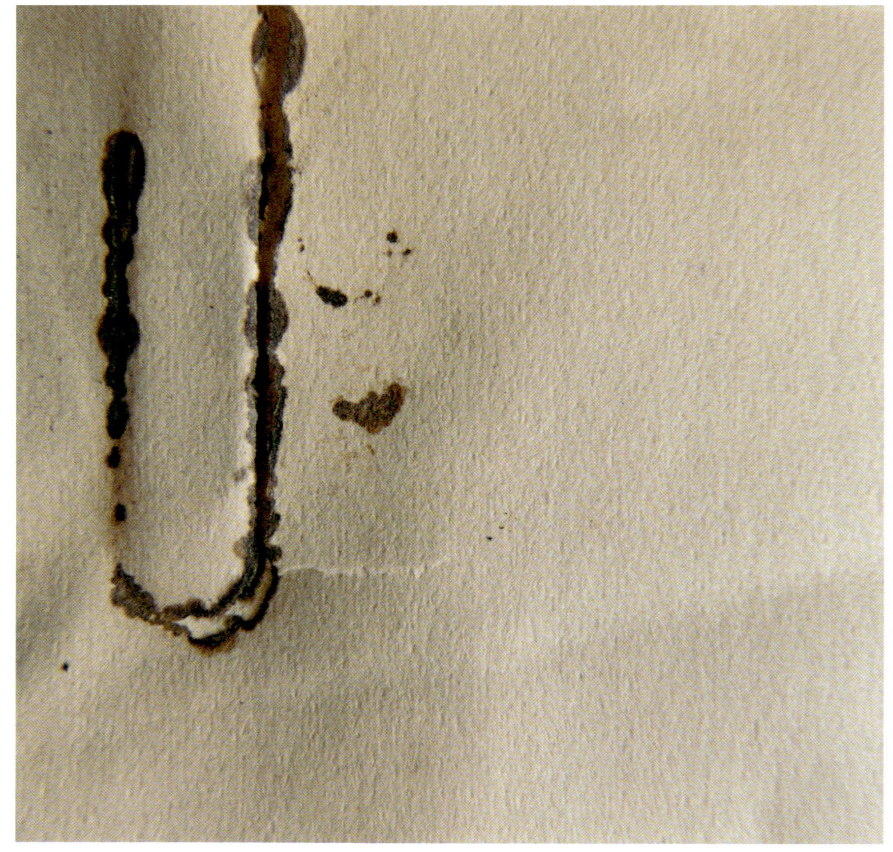

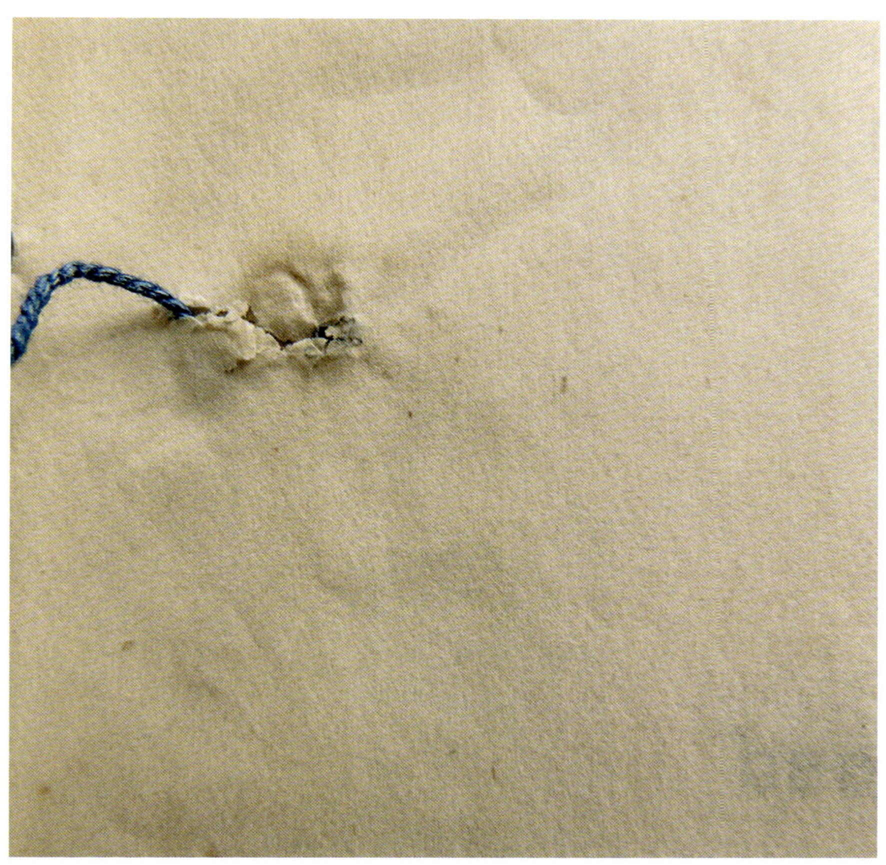

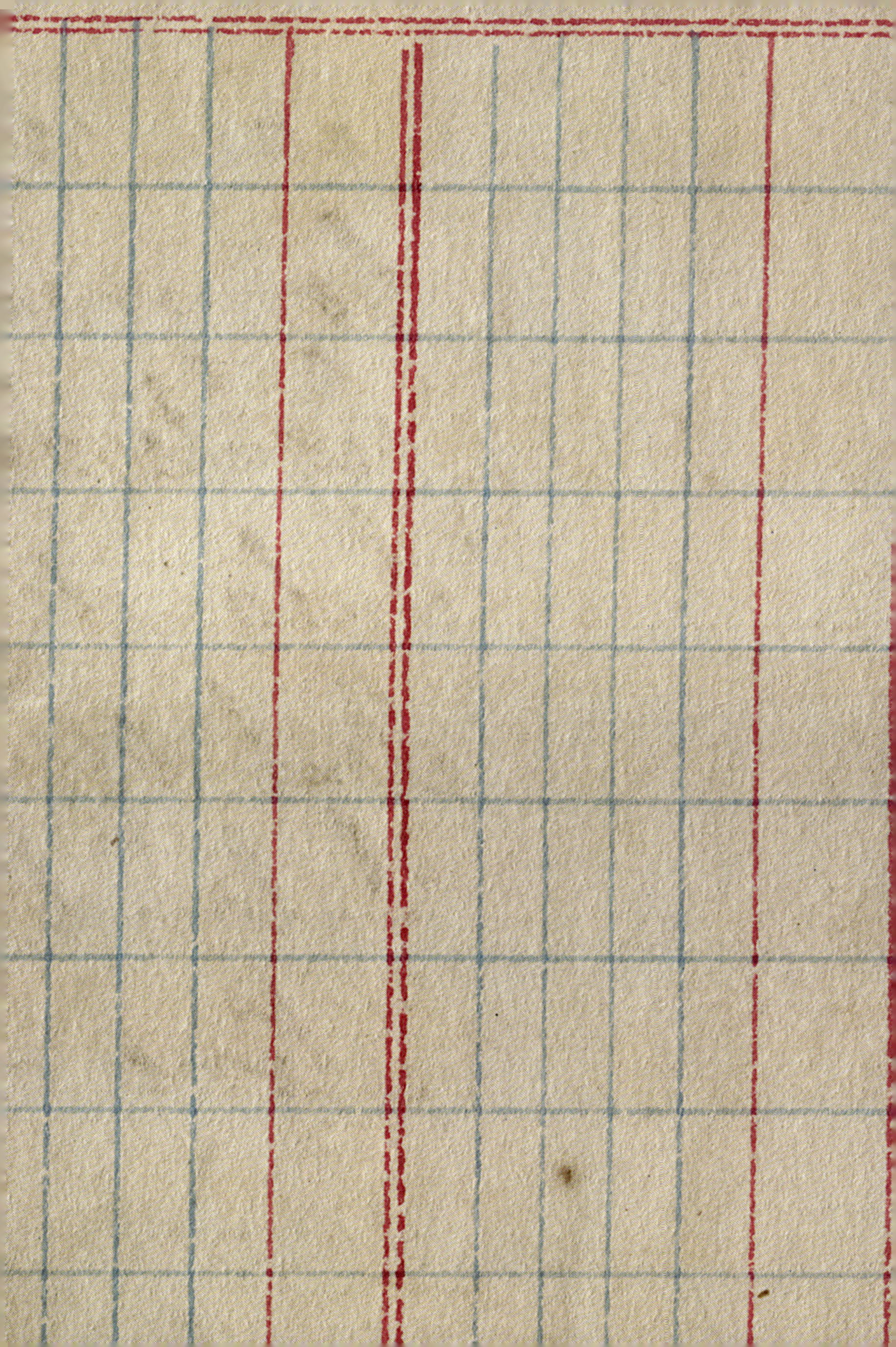

Book of Free Slaves
/11/91

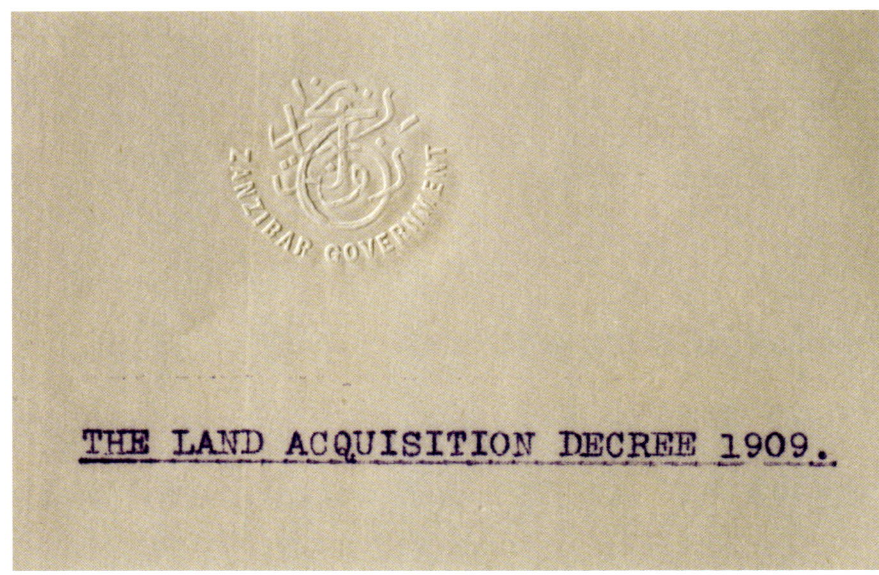

ZANZIBAR GOVERNMENT
THE LAND ACQUISITION DECREE 1909.

SURCHARGE IN
BLACK ONLY

On Fatima's first visit to the archives she took her camera, all the while thinking about the postcards. One of the women in the postcards suggested that she look through the court documents of HM Agent and Consul-General in the archives, in the probate and administration, declarations and petitions of executors. The names, dates, Gujarati writing, stamps, string, letters in English and Gujarati translations – they were all very beautifully written. Then there was the texture of the paper. Everything was written on a very fine, thin paper. The paper creased the writing. Some of the written Gujarati had distinct graphite qualities, shiny like gunpowder. There was Arabic text too. The writing, words, texture, embossing – all enlarged inside the camera with a very close-up lens. The writing reads:

> Formerly under the dual government of Great Britain, in 1894
> the administration was ceded to the latter, Land Decree

The postcards whispered, 'At a certain moment, the goalposts were moved.' Women could not own property. The government tried to seize as many properties as it could. Fatima was reminded of a lecture in her first year at university on the Brontë sisters and *Wuthering Heights*. She kept hearing and thinking about what it means if women can't own property. It was as if she had been stung by a bee. The going backwards and forwards caused a commotion in the archives. Fatima wanted to understand the history of women being able to own property. The postcard spoke again, 'I am illiterate. English is the only language allowed. How do I argue my case?' Fatima was looking at first-hand records.

'This archive is unique,' she thought to herself. What is the psychology behind these documents? What ideologies are contained within them? What do they tell us about Britain and Europe culturally? Can the archive tell us anything more? What has changed?

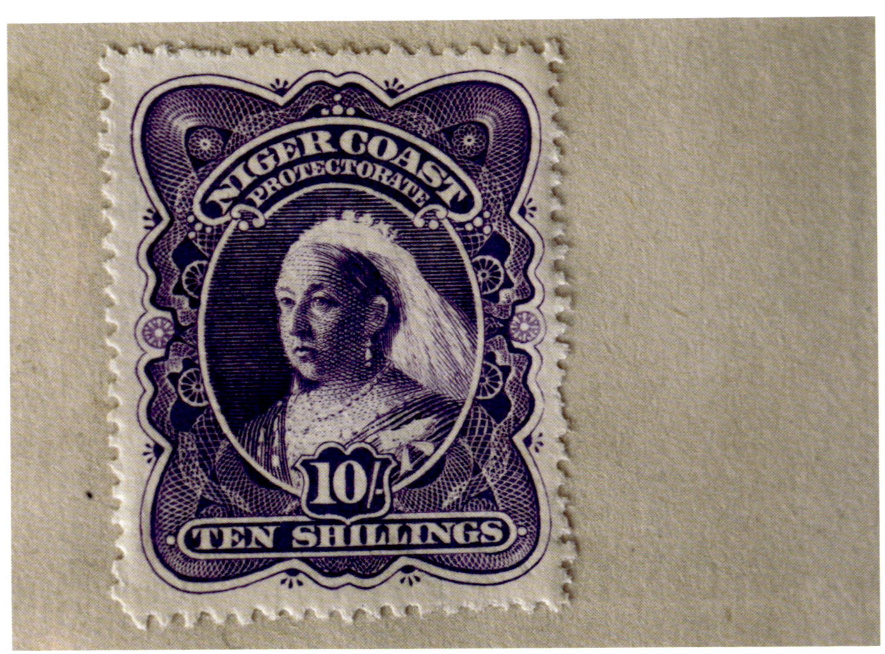

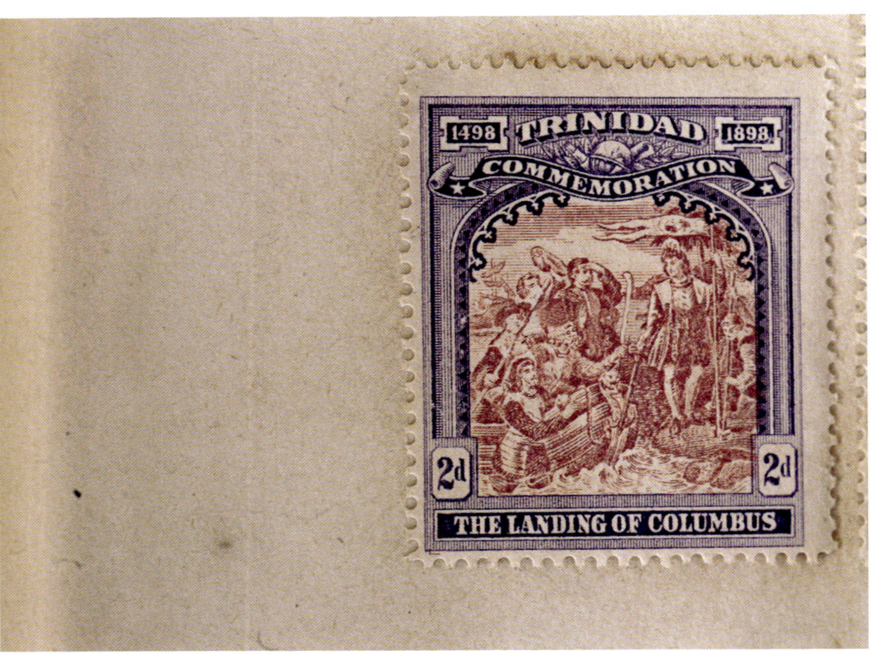

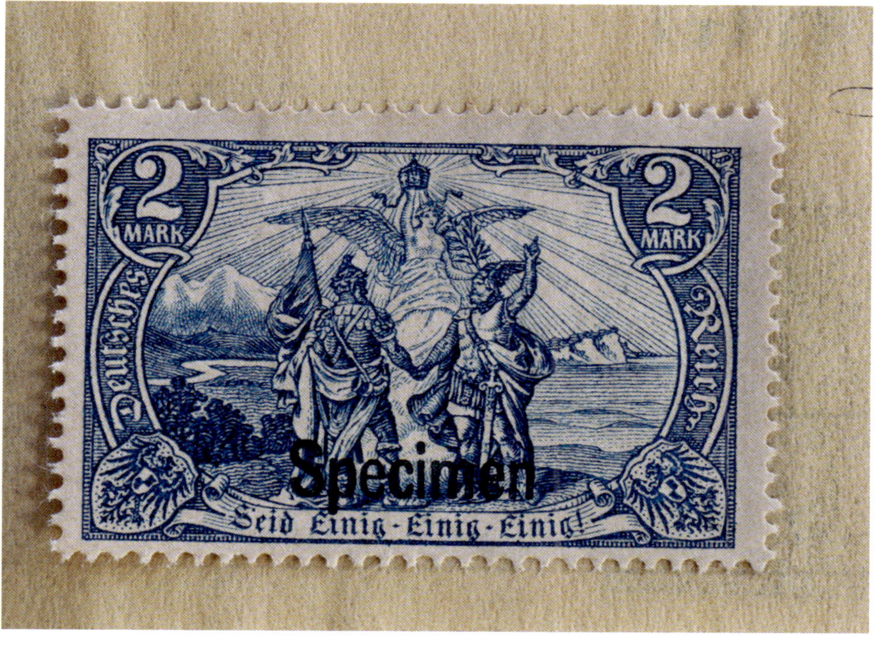2
MARK
2
MARK
Deutsches
Reich
Specimen
Seid Einig · Einig · Einig!

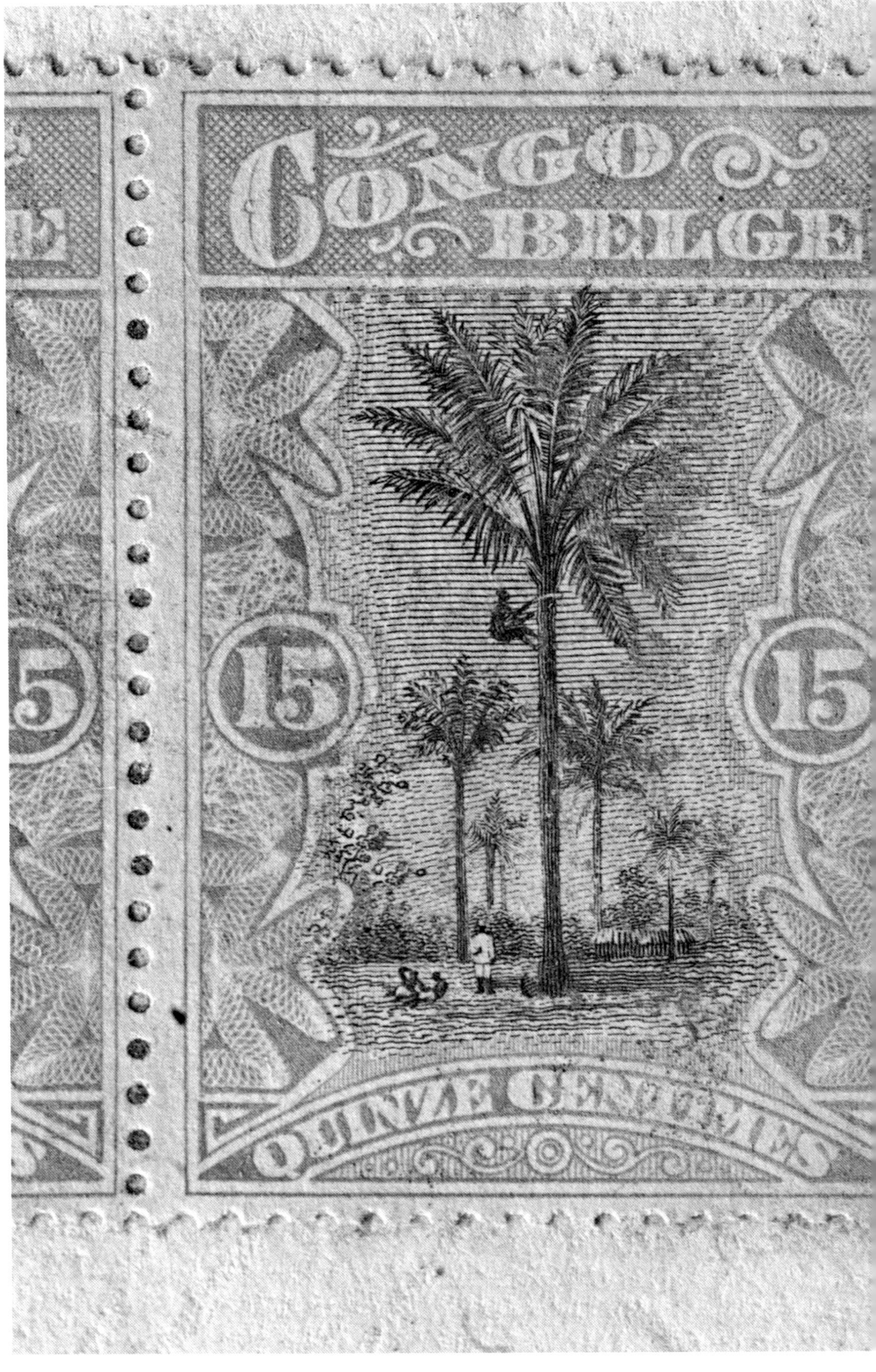

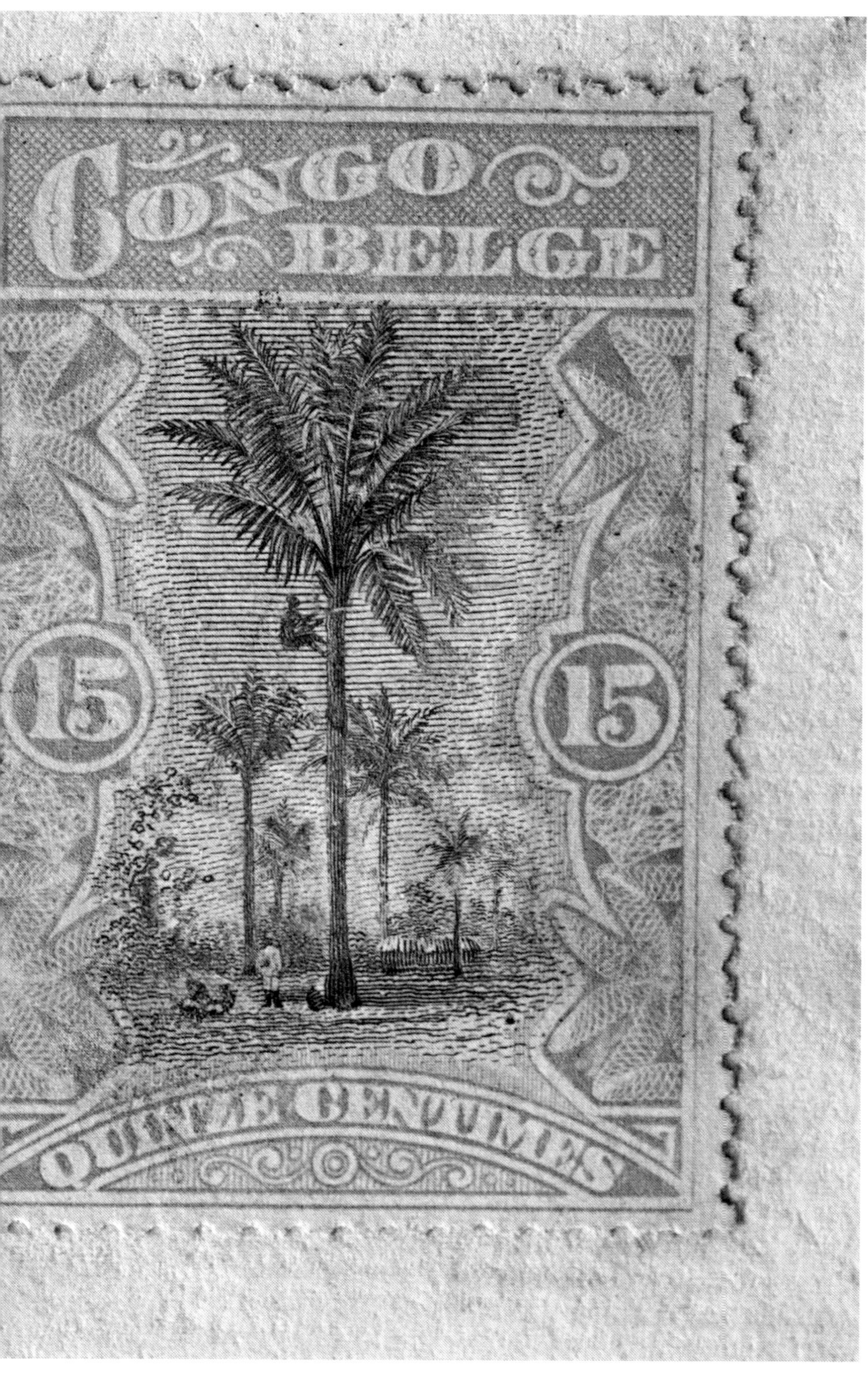

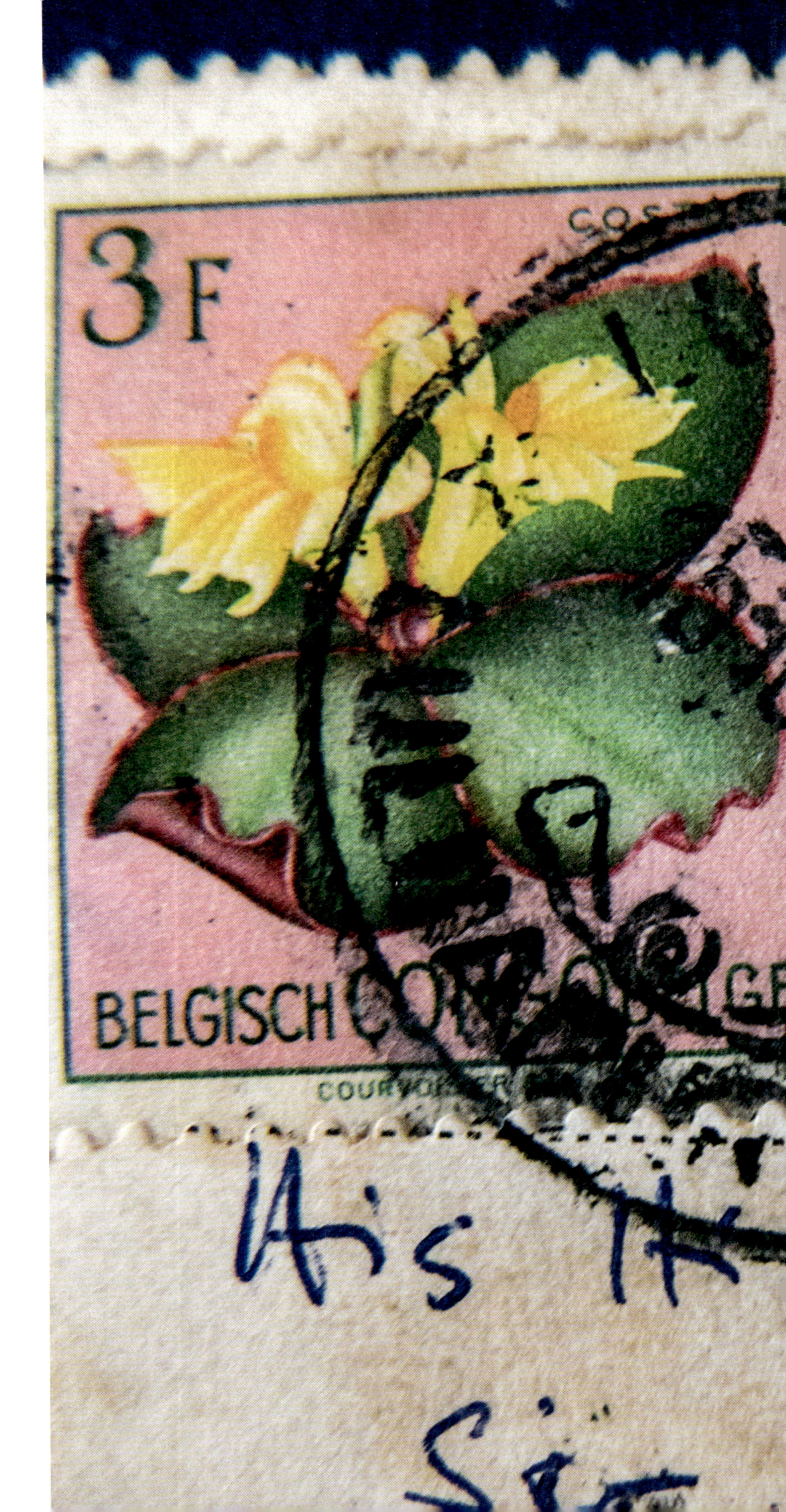
3 F
BELGISCH CONGO
COURVOISIER

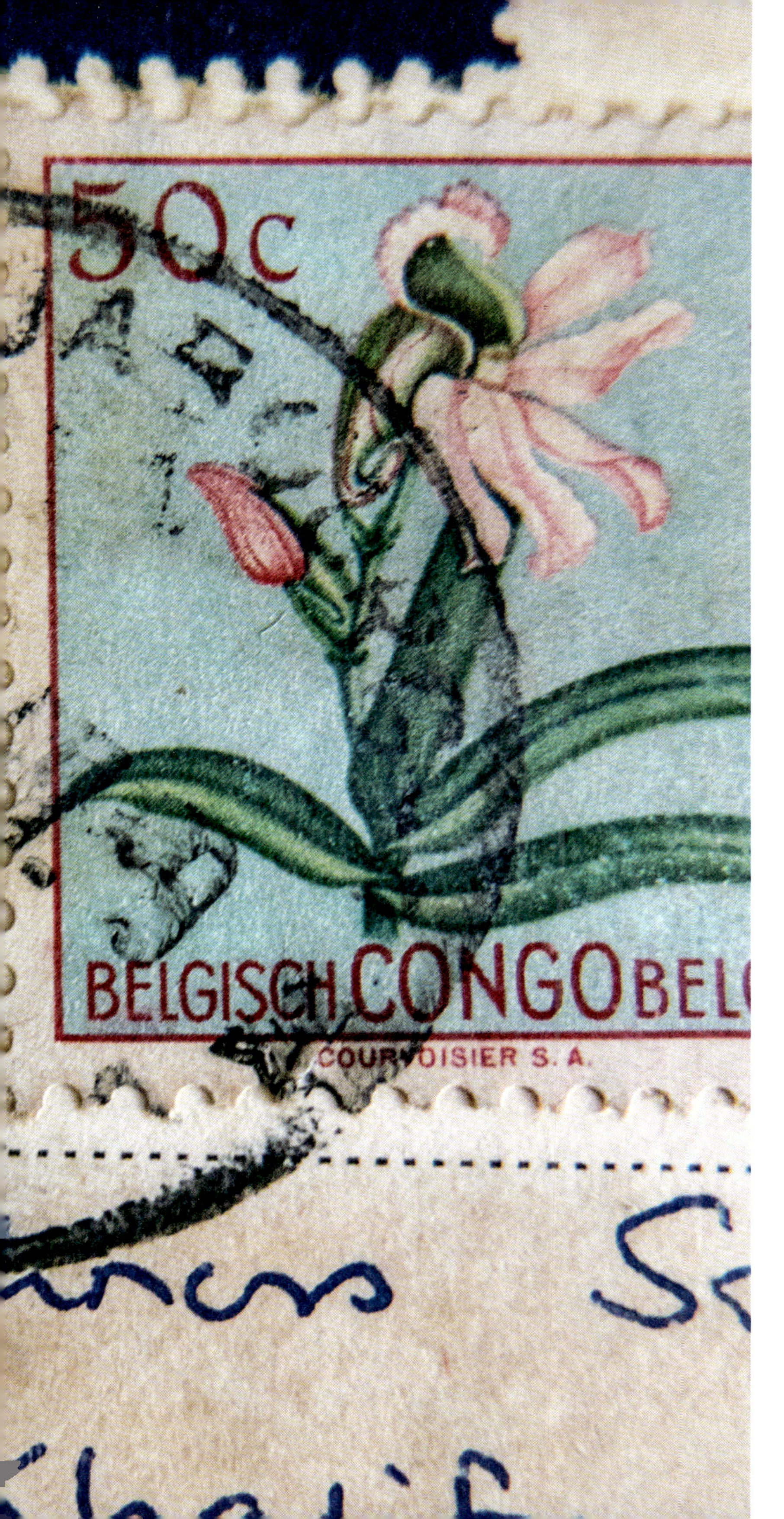

50 c
BELGISCH CONGO BEL
COURVOISIER S.A.

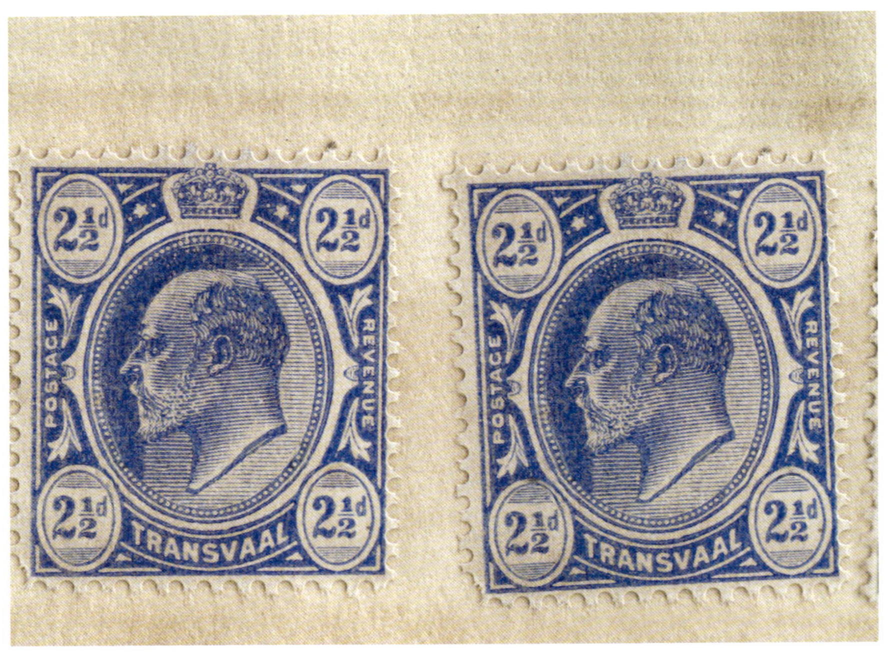

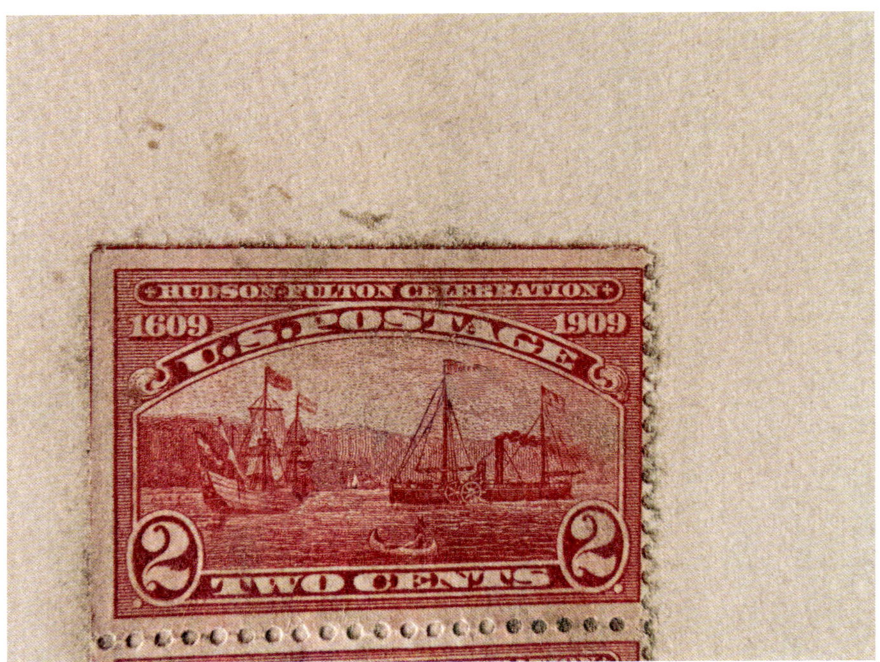
HUDSON · FULTON · CELEBRATION
1609 U.S. POSTAGE 1909
TWO CENTS
2
2

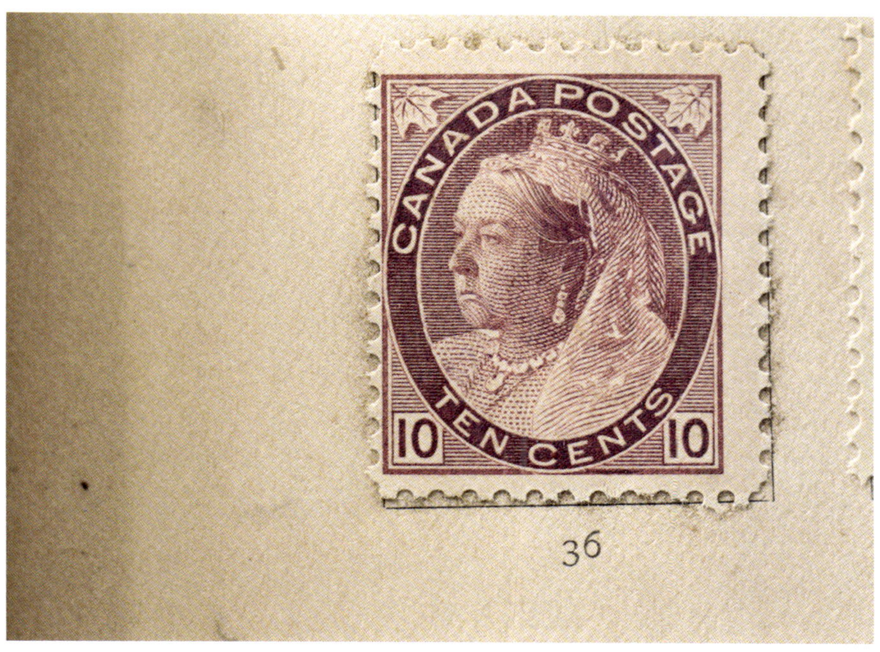

36

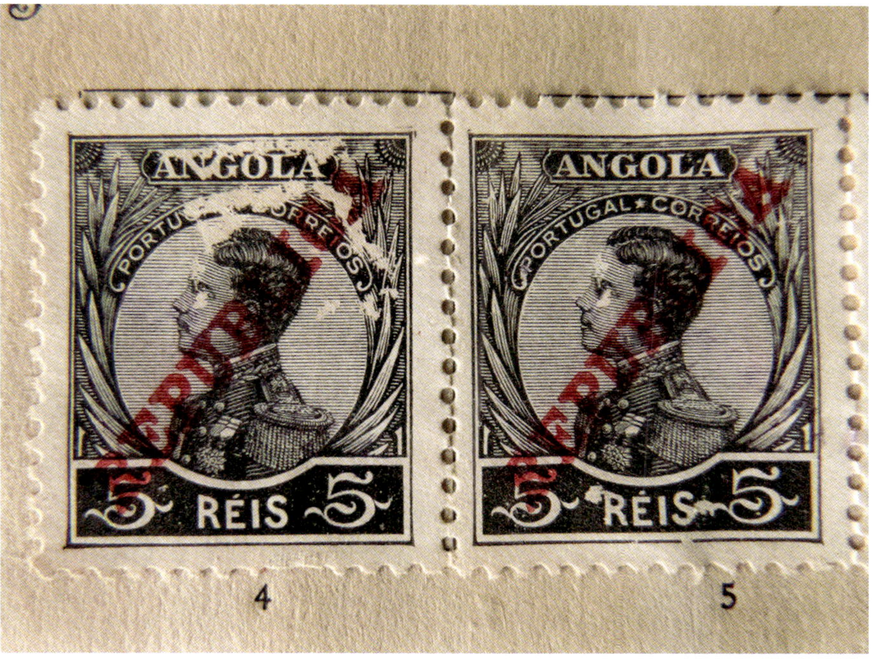

4 5

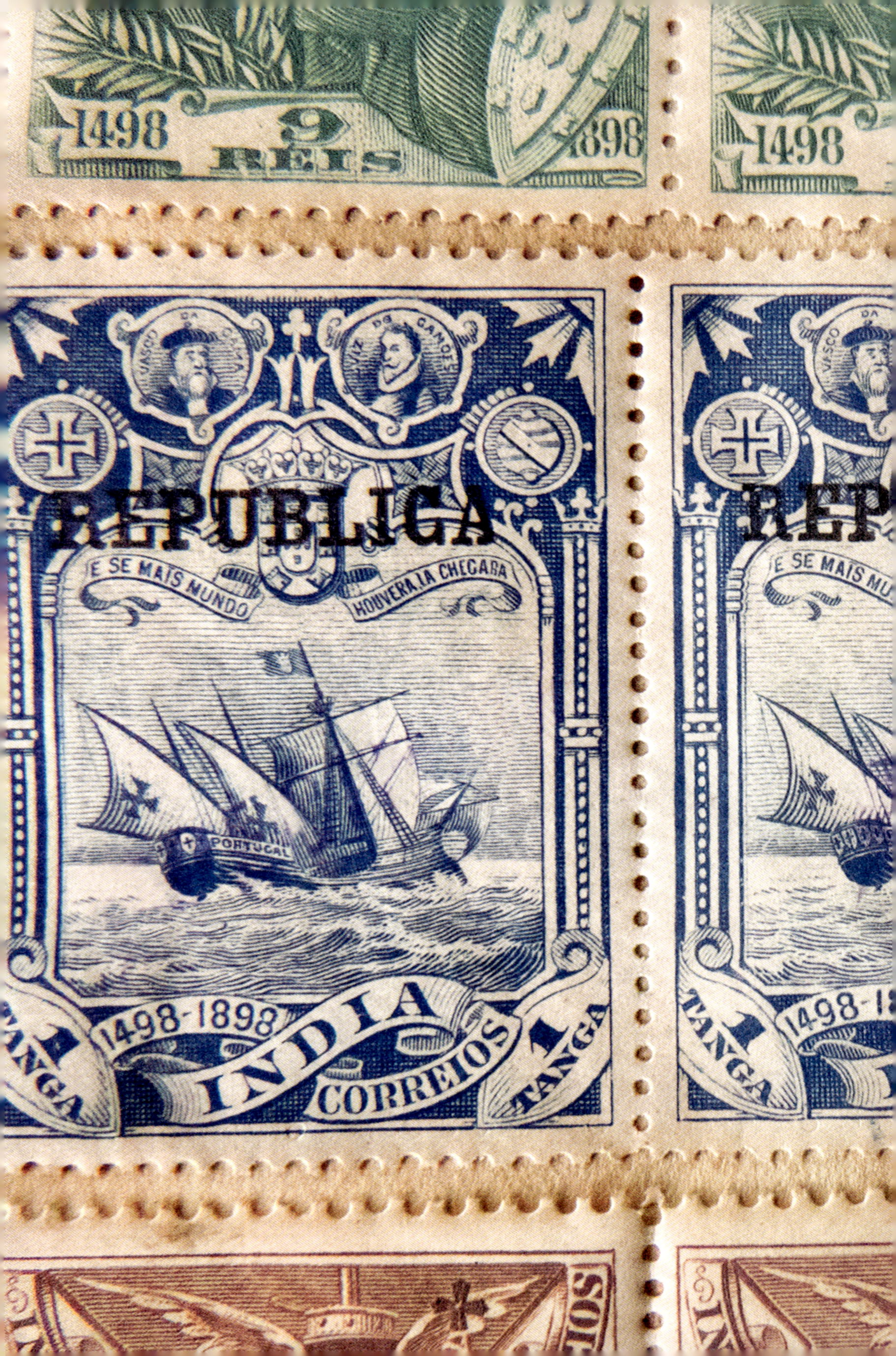

1498
2 REIS
1898
1498
1898
VASCO DA GAMA
LVIZ DE CAMÕES
REPUBLICA
E SE MAIS MUNDO HOUVERA LA CHEGARA
PORTUGAL
1 TANGA
1498-1898
INDIA
CORREIOS
1 TANGA
VASCO DA
REP
E SE MAIS MU
1 TANGA
1498-18

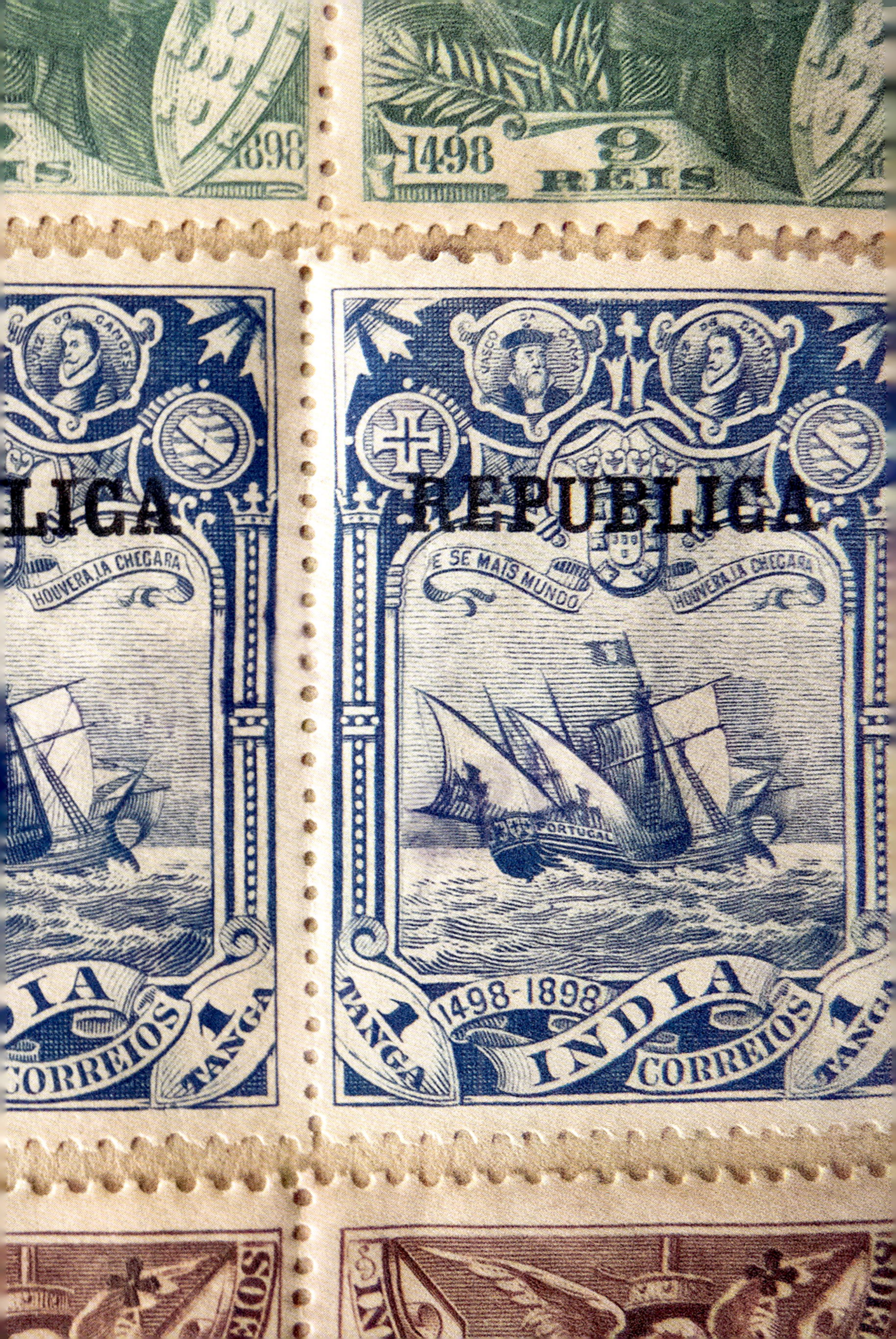

1498
1498
9 REIS
REPUBLICA
REPUBLICA
E SE MAIS MUNDO
HOUVERA LA CHEGARA
HOUVERA LA CHEGARA
PORTUGAL
1498-1898
INDIA
CORREIOS
TANGA
1
TANGA
INDIA
CORREIOS

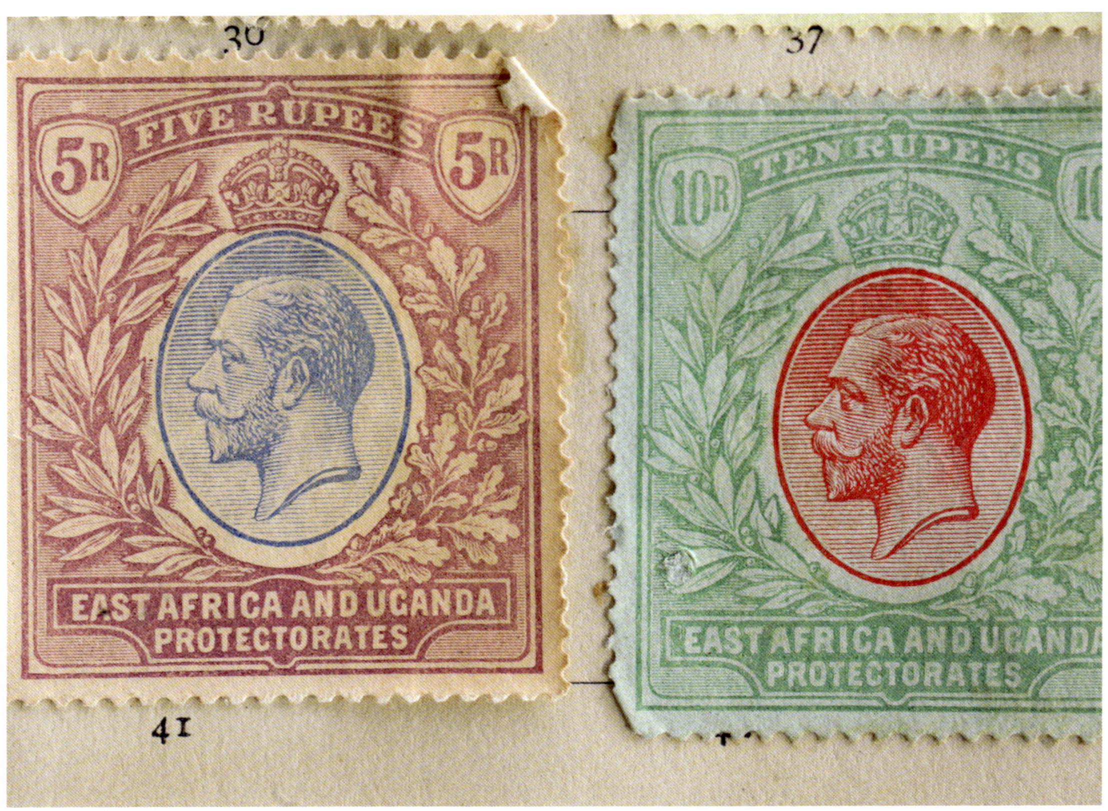
30
5R FIVE RUPEES 5R
EAST AFRICA AND UGANDA
PROTECTORATES
41
37
10R TEN RUPEES 10
EAST AFRICA AND UGANDA
PROTECTORATES

20

19

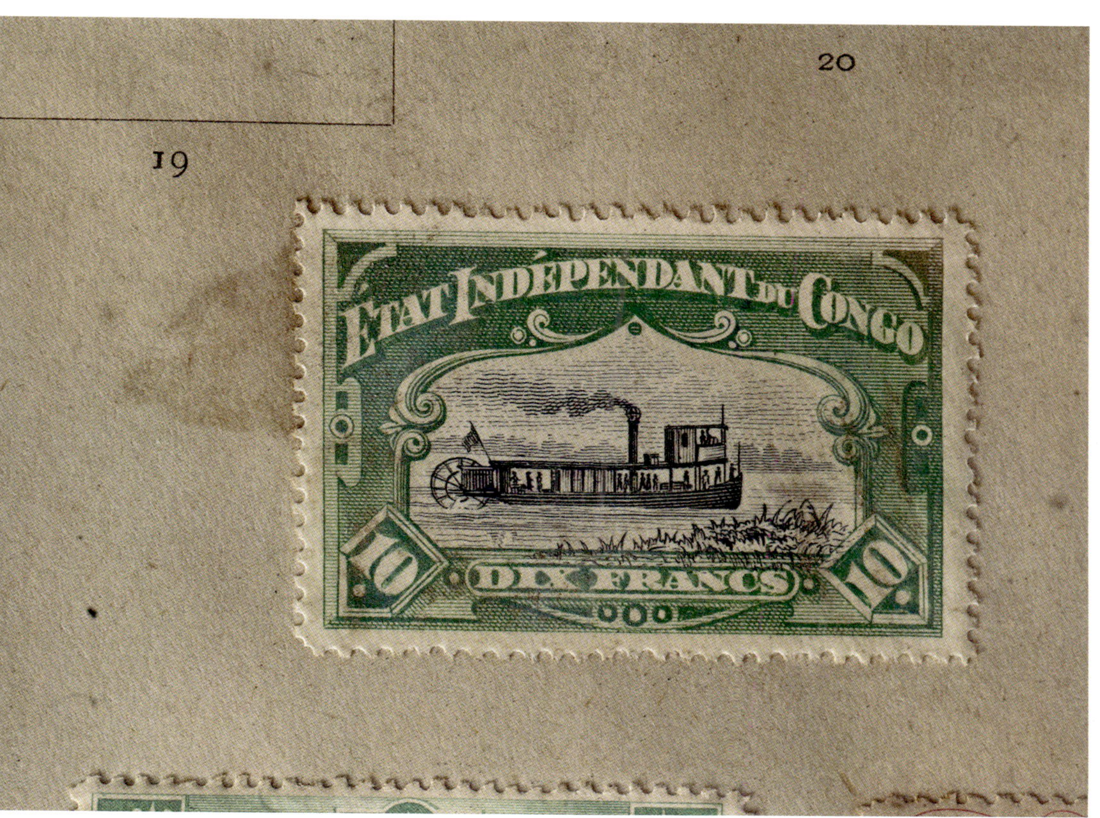

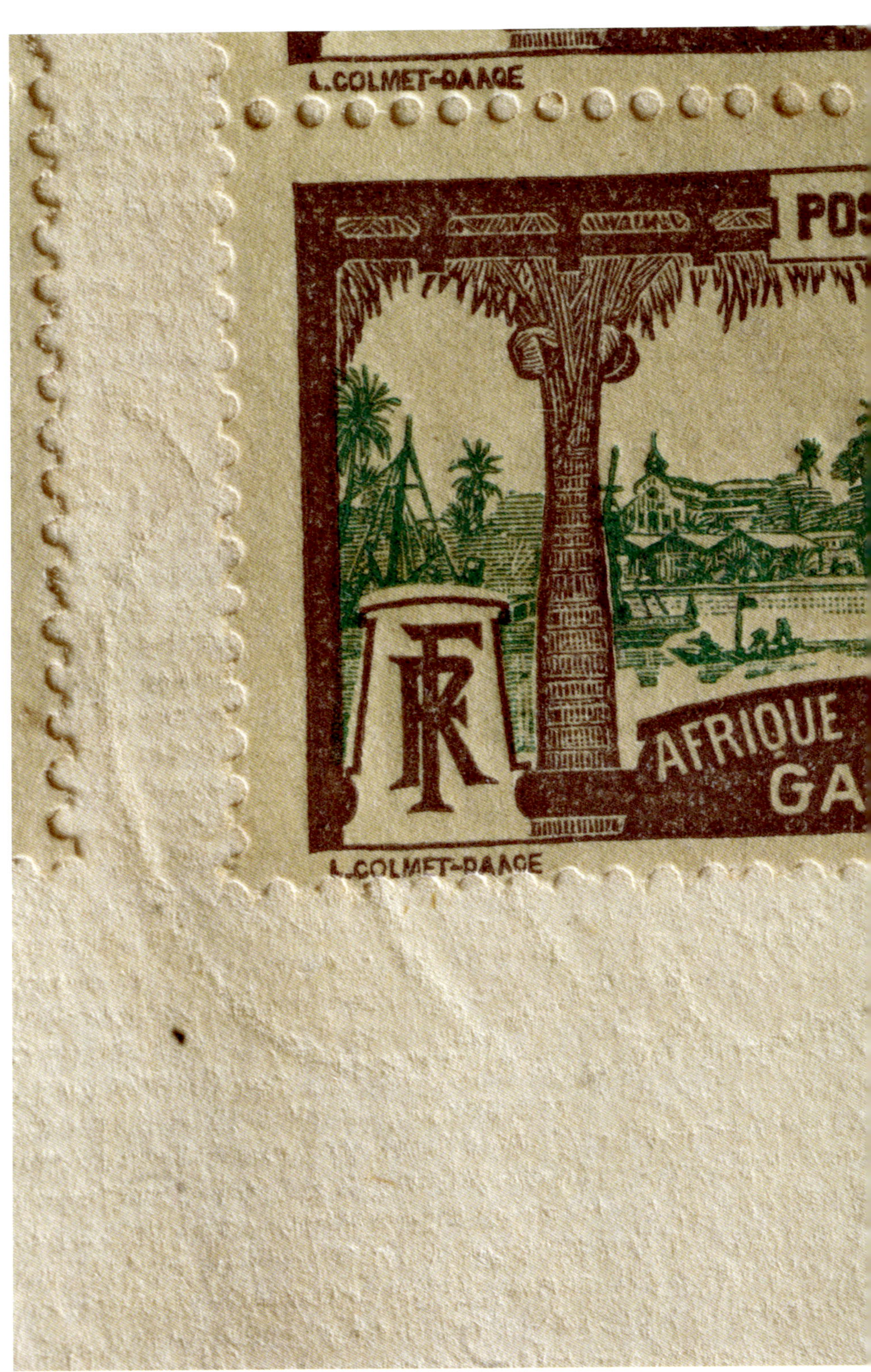
L. COLMET-DAAGE
POS
AFRIQUE
GA
L. COLMET-DAAGE

102   103

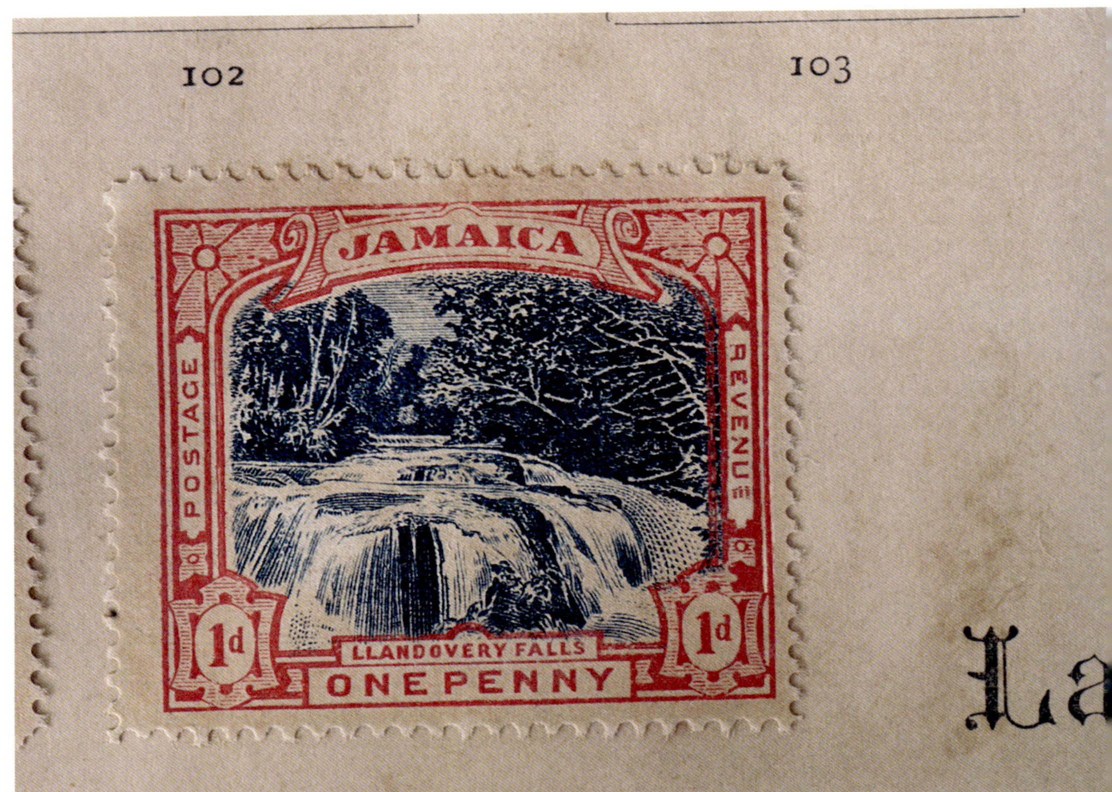

La

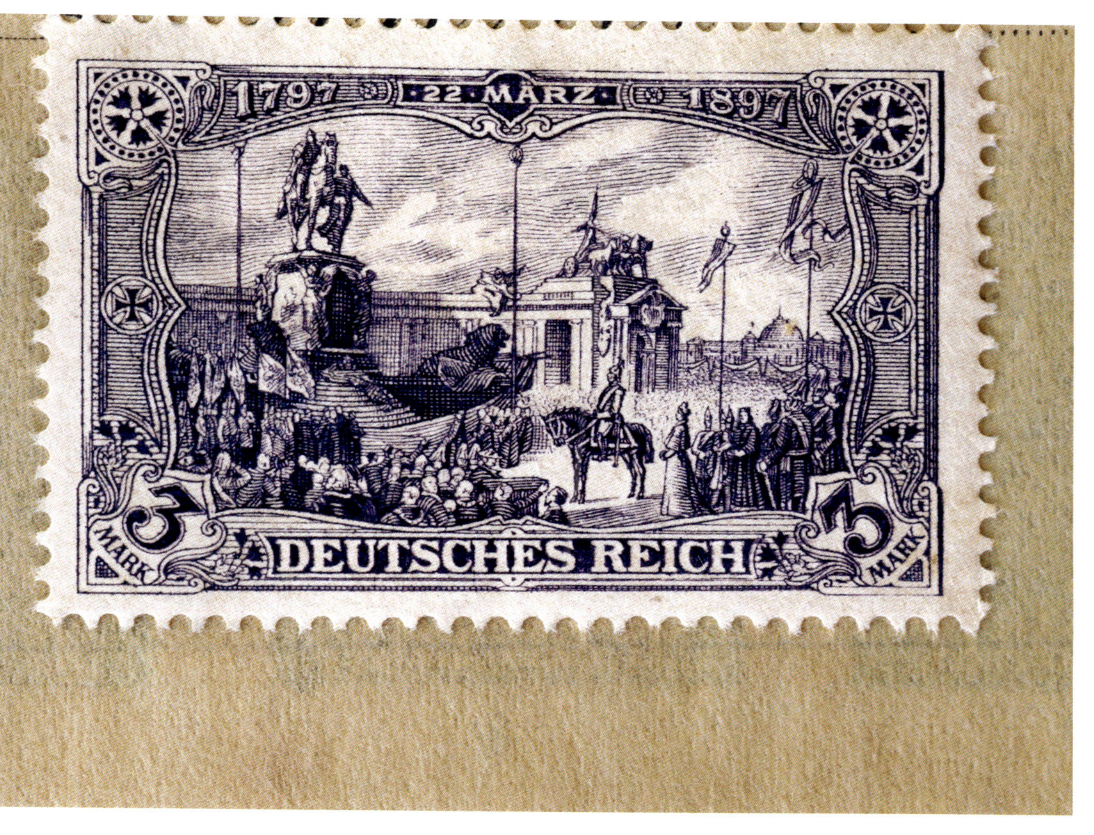

1797 · 22 MÄRZ · 1897
DEUTSCHES REICH
3 MARK
3 MARK

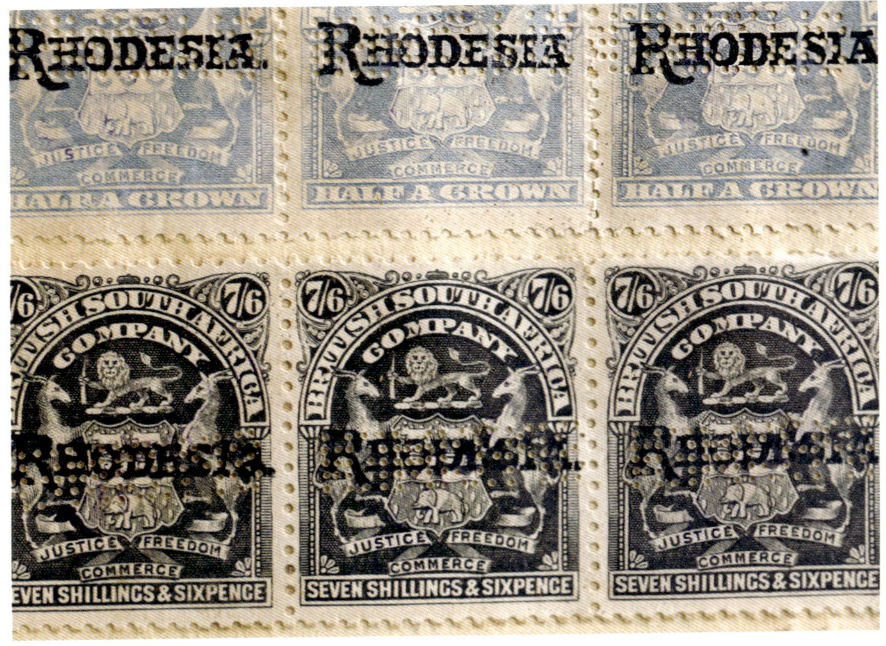

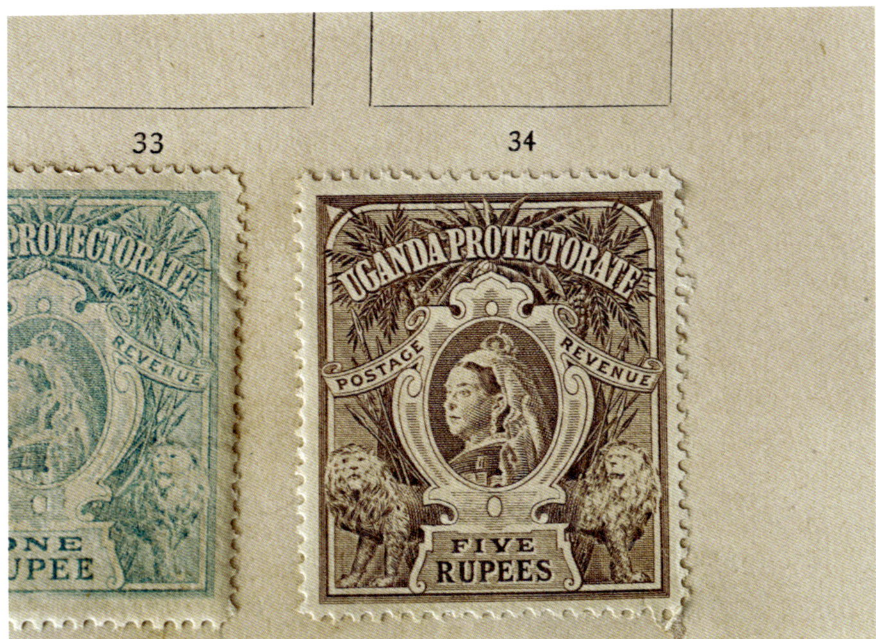

33
34

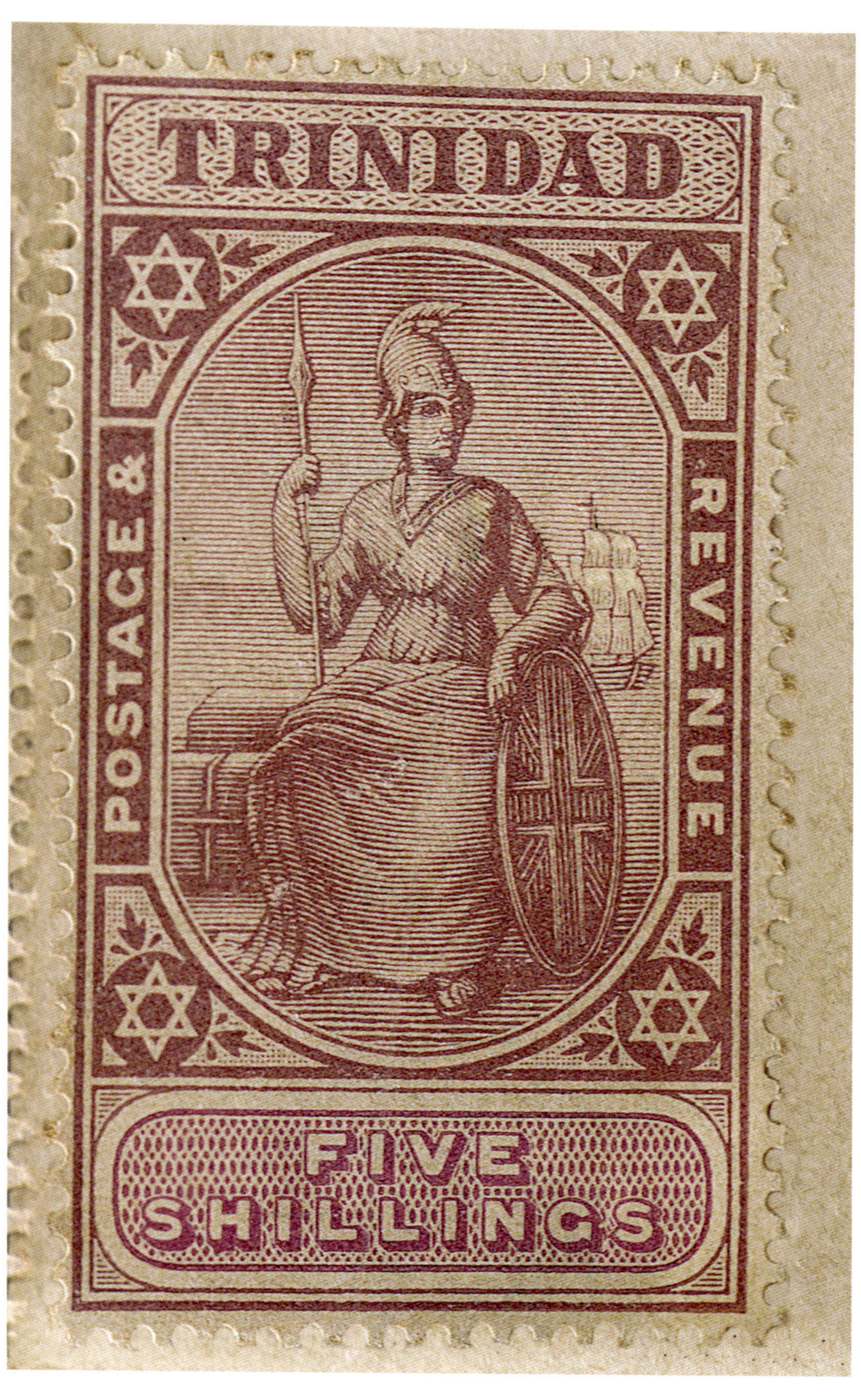

TRINIDAD
POSTAGE &
REVENUE
FIVE
SHILLINGS

5s SLATE BLUE

The streets are infused with the melancholy of decay. Their house was on the crest of Cinnamon Hill – 25 acres of tropical garden idyll. There were spectacular, Italian-inspired views over the lake and tropical jungle. The courtyard, the pavilions and the paths leading to a multitude of views only served to emphasise the beauty of the gardens.

The rooms were made for this hot, humid zone. The view was of swaying palm trees, enduring bouts of burning equatorial sun followed by the relentless beating rain.

Newly independent countries adopted international modernism, taking inspiration from the ancient. After independence was a great time for optimism and experimentation. People were open to new ideas. Even though resources were limited, anything seemed possible because of their newfound freedom. After some time, however, everything changed.

Fatima wanted to understand what the 1964 Zanzibar revolution was. Not in words but visually; such subjects were never aired publicly, but in private people she met confided in her. They asked her not to mention it to anybody. She started to photograph the cars in the museum where she had bought the postcards many years ago. That was when she met the late Mr Omar Kibao. He was a curator. They would talk a lot. He often used the Swahili phrase *sisi tuko moja* (we are one). Fatima wondered if these words could become an object, and if so, could the curator curate this object? They talked very openly. The words took a while to arrive. How to understand hatred, to understand racial segregation. The British club had two sets of stairs. Only those who belonged to the British Crown were permitted. Fatima asked herself, 'Am I allowed to love an African man?' This thought lay unconscious for many years, until one sunny morning it came to her again as she was walking up the stairs to her bedroom. She understood that she had held her heart tight. The moment she understood this there came a deep warmth in heart. She was free to love whomsoever she wanted. During the revolution it got messy.

There was a loss of passion, desire and drive in the streets.

Every afternoon after the archives had closed Fatima would sit with an elderly businessman called Sherali. Fatima asked, 'Was it all too alien, too foreign, or were people just afraid?' He replied to her, 'Did you know the *coup d'état* of 18–20 January led to the massacre of between five and 20,000 Arabs and Indians whose families had been living in Zanzibar for centuries?' She had been told that the revolution was basically a communist revolt. Also that it had racial underpinnings, and it was this that had led to the massacre of Arabs and Indians. Thousands more people fled in fear and their houses were confiscated by the State. Revolution was hardly mentioned in the archive. Fatima wanted to go home when she realised that the archive itself was contributing to this history of ethnic cleansing. Her body felt weak. The next day she asked the camera, 'What is an archive and how does it order?' The camera allowed her to blow up words huge. She wanted to play with scale so the words could scream, shout, object. Using multiple shots, through editing and by working with individual photos, she hoped to create a kind of musical score. The embroidery had a beauty – the colours, silk threads, ribbons, chain stitches, cross stitches, the cotton, the linen. There was similar cotton in the postcards. It reminded her of calligraphy, of Damascus, Cairo, Istanbul, the Mughal emperor Akbar, Lahore, Agra, Fatehpur, Ahmedabad and the Industrial Revolution.

This au—

could not be

expenses of

of British

of British co

ority, however

eld to cover the

e despatch

bjects, natives

ries to Bombay,

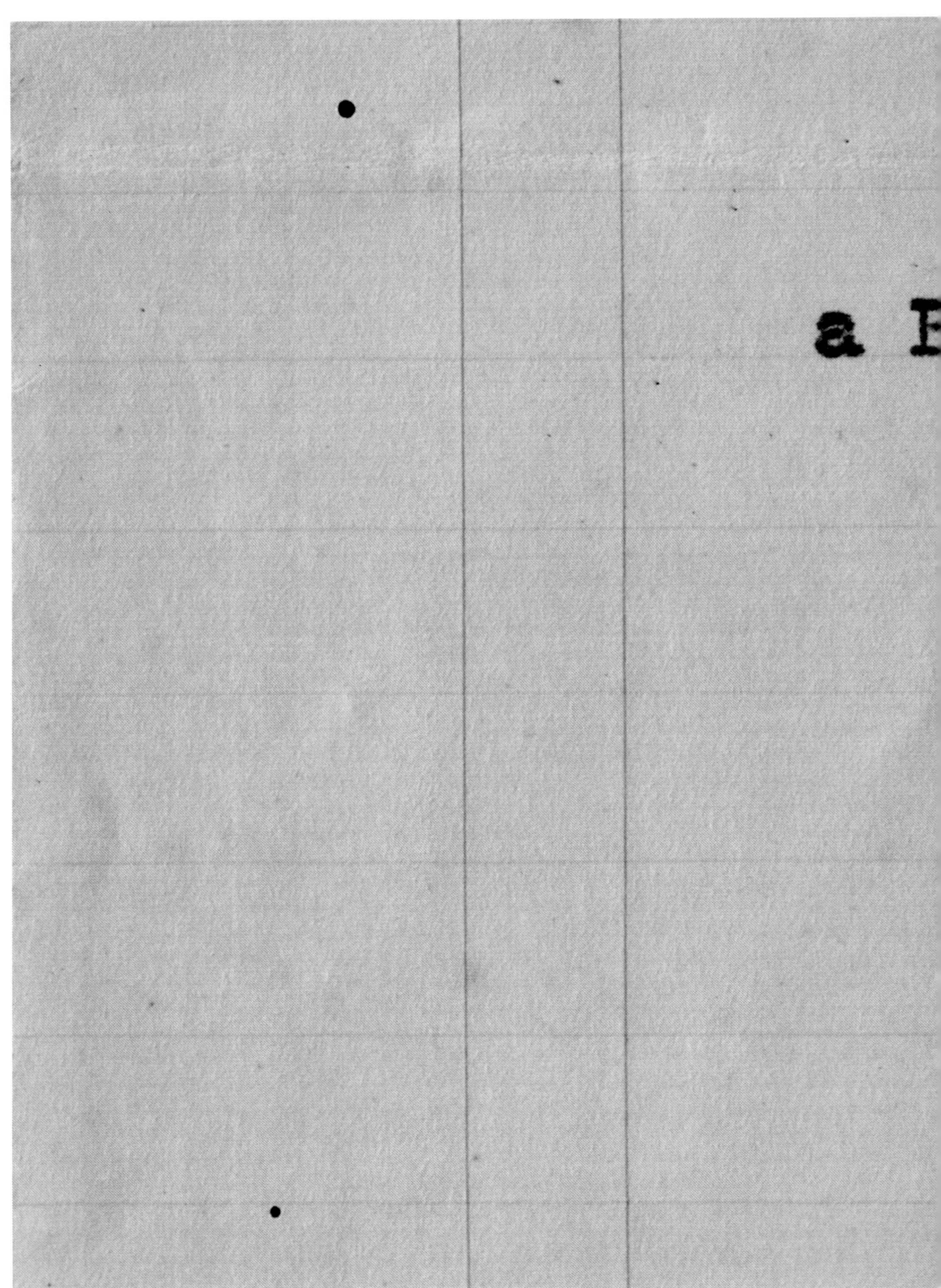

tish Subject,

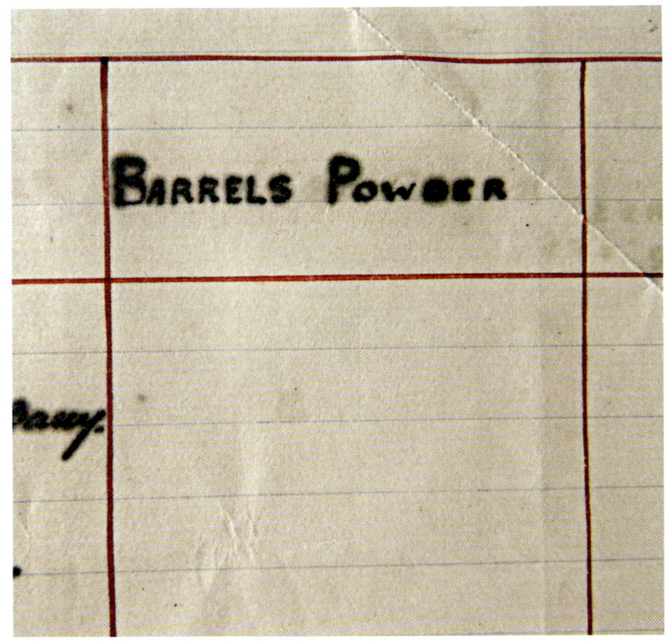
BARRELS POWDER

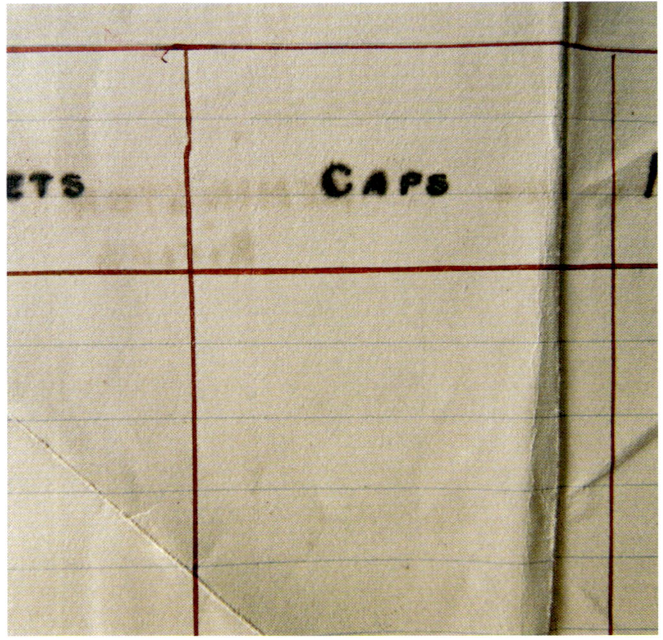
ETS
CAPS

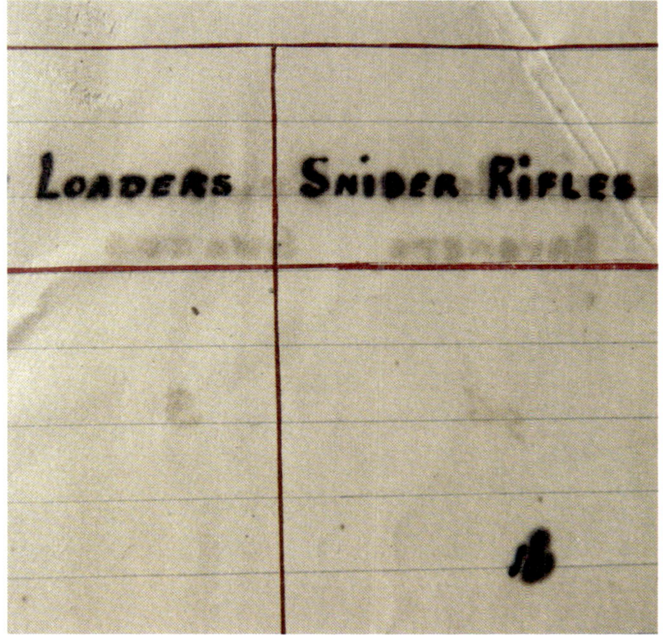

MAXIM GUN
MAXIM CARTRIDGES
LOADERS
SNIDER RIFLES

RULES

Fatima decides she would like to become a historian of visual culture. She is shocked that all of these countries could be taken over by Europe. It was assumed that this was completely normal at the time, and it is this that is so shocking. Fatima wants to focus on the psychology of the documents in the archives. The camera is a witness, it records. How are ideologies driven by institutions? What are individual ideologies? It becomes like a set of photographs that are similar but that build up into many, creating a louder sound, like a musical score. Juxtaposing different attitudes, they create patterns. When you see one it is clearly different from the others, but when you see thousands, they become a singular image. It has to do with culture. When images are repeated they become something else, and here, if we choose to look, attitudes, gestures and shadows can be found.

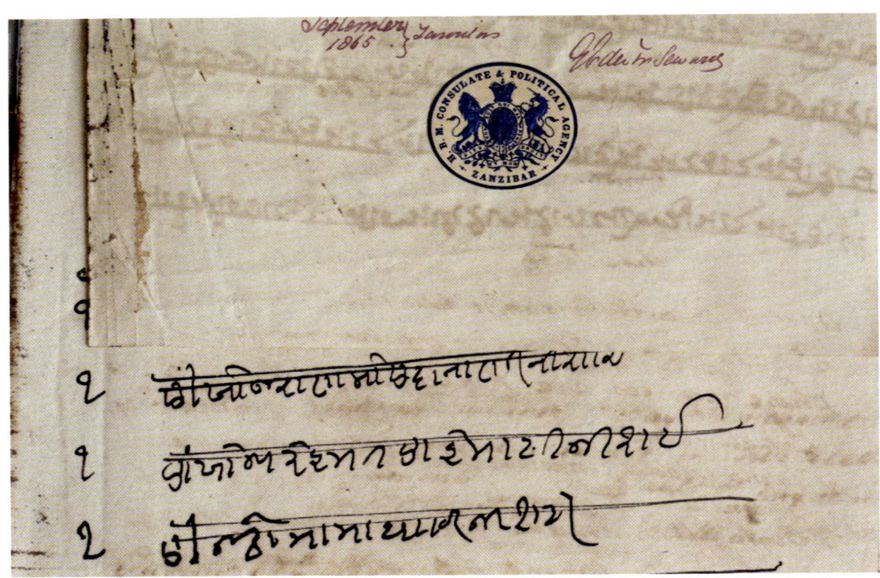

country,under our authority,

                    ,therefore,induced the Sultan,by a purely

arbitrary act,to free the slaves." no compensation was paid

to the owners.Under certain treaties,Great Britain had

certain extra-territorial rights and the Sultan could not

touch British subjects,who were amenable solely to the

jurisdiction of the British Consulate.The Indians were

British subjects and I claimed,therefore,that Great Britain

had the right to prevent their carrying on the slave trade.

The measure was attended with most gratifying success.

    The Indians became loyal subjects of the British Crown,

having no motive,other than loyal subjects and knowing that

Great Britain could effectually protect them against the

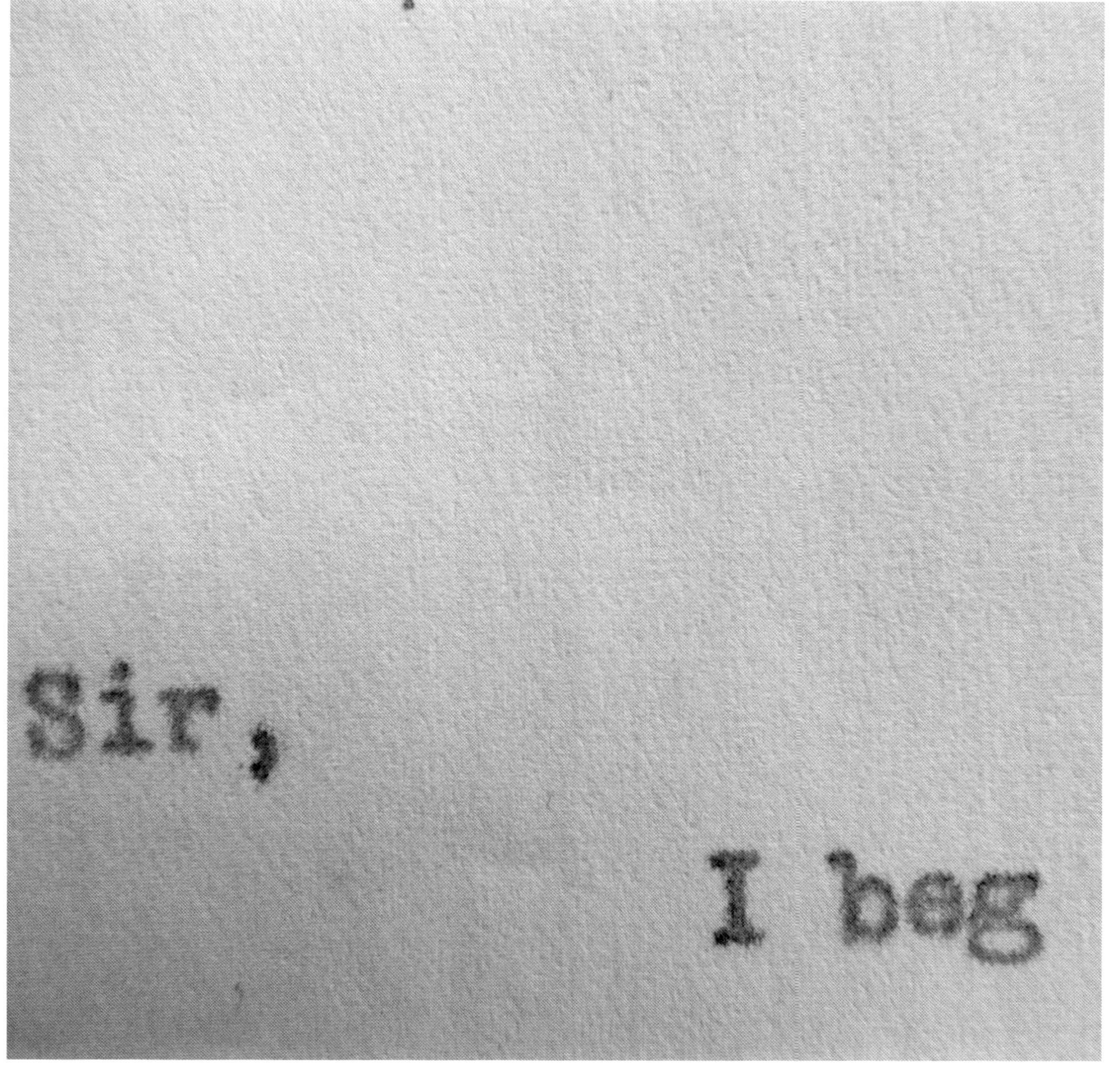
Sir,
I beg

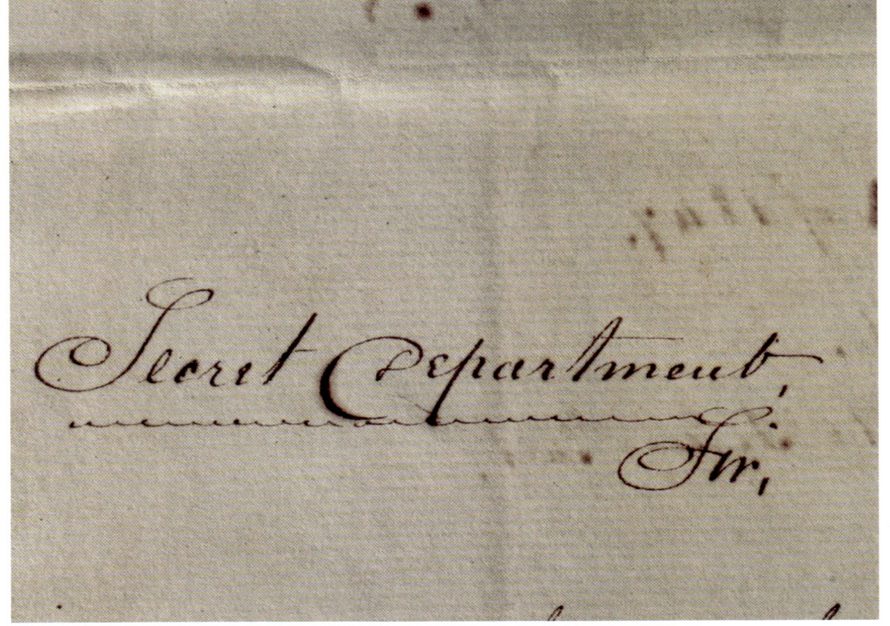

The Colonial Office is sorely puzzled to know what to do with the slaves rescued by our cruisers on the east coast of Africa. There is no Sierra Leone there, with the double advantage of a British Government and a kindred population, nor is there any place within easy reach where they can escape the risk of being smuggled back into slavery or else dying from starvation. In its embarrassment the Office has lately determined to send the freed slaves to Zanzibar itself, and to give them on landing a printed certificate of freedom, with a right of appeal to the British Consul. Dr. —— (who knows Zanzibar well), writes to the *Mission Life* in strong terms, observing that "it would be better to abandon all attempts to stop the slave trade altogether than to enact such a mockery as this." He draws a picture of the way in which the scheme will work :—

A large slave dhow has been taken, and the slaves are being brought on shore ; there will be 200 or 300 poor naked creatures, with never more than a very little piece of very dirty rag round their middles ; at least half of them have some kind of eruption on the skin ; all are very much emaciated, a few dozen scarcely able to walk ; some suffering from dysentery, and one or two from small-pox. What is to become of them all ? The English consul has no money ; but he has plenty of certificates of freedom. He tries to make out a list, and asks their names. There are thirty Mabrukis and five-and-twenty Songolos, and so on with the other common slave names. It is simply impossible that any human being should know them all again.

To turn these poor creatures adrift with a bit of paper of which they neither understand the meaning nor the use, is merely to offer them one of two alternatives—to lie down and die, or to go to the slave market and be sold. Dr. —— contends that if we do not wish to stultify ourselves, the British consul should at any rate be empowered to give them a few yards of calico and a few days' shelter and food. If money for these purposes be found, the English and French missions will take on themselves much of the responsibility for the care of these freedmen, and the internal slave trade would receive an immediate check.

AFRICA.

GENERA

OF

CONFERENCE

SINGNED FEB

3   1886

ACT

E

OF BERLIN

RY 26, 1885

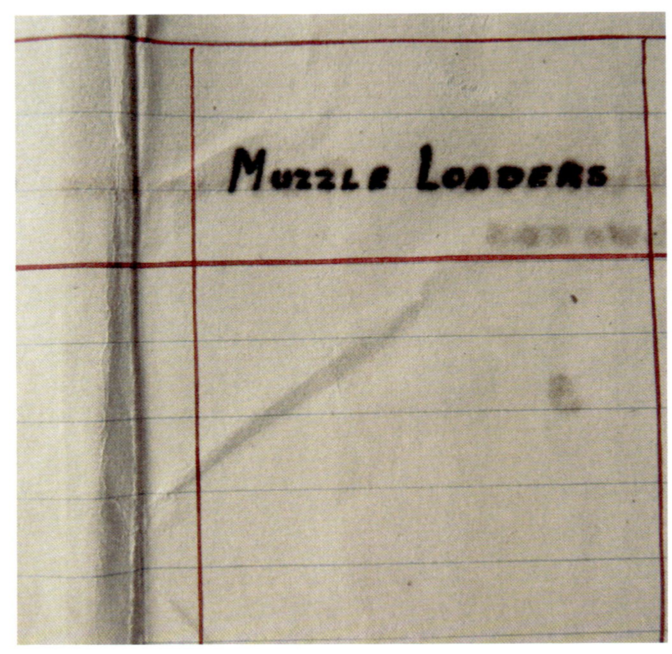

MUZZLE LOADERS

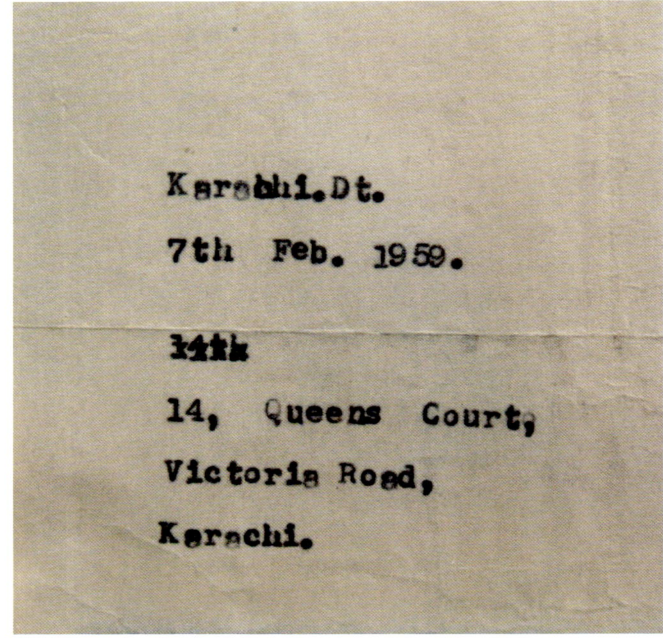

Karachi.Dt.
7th Feb. 1959.
14th
14, Queens Court,
Victoria Road,
Karachi.

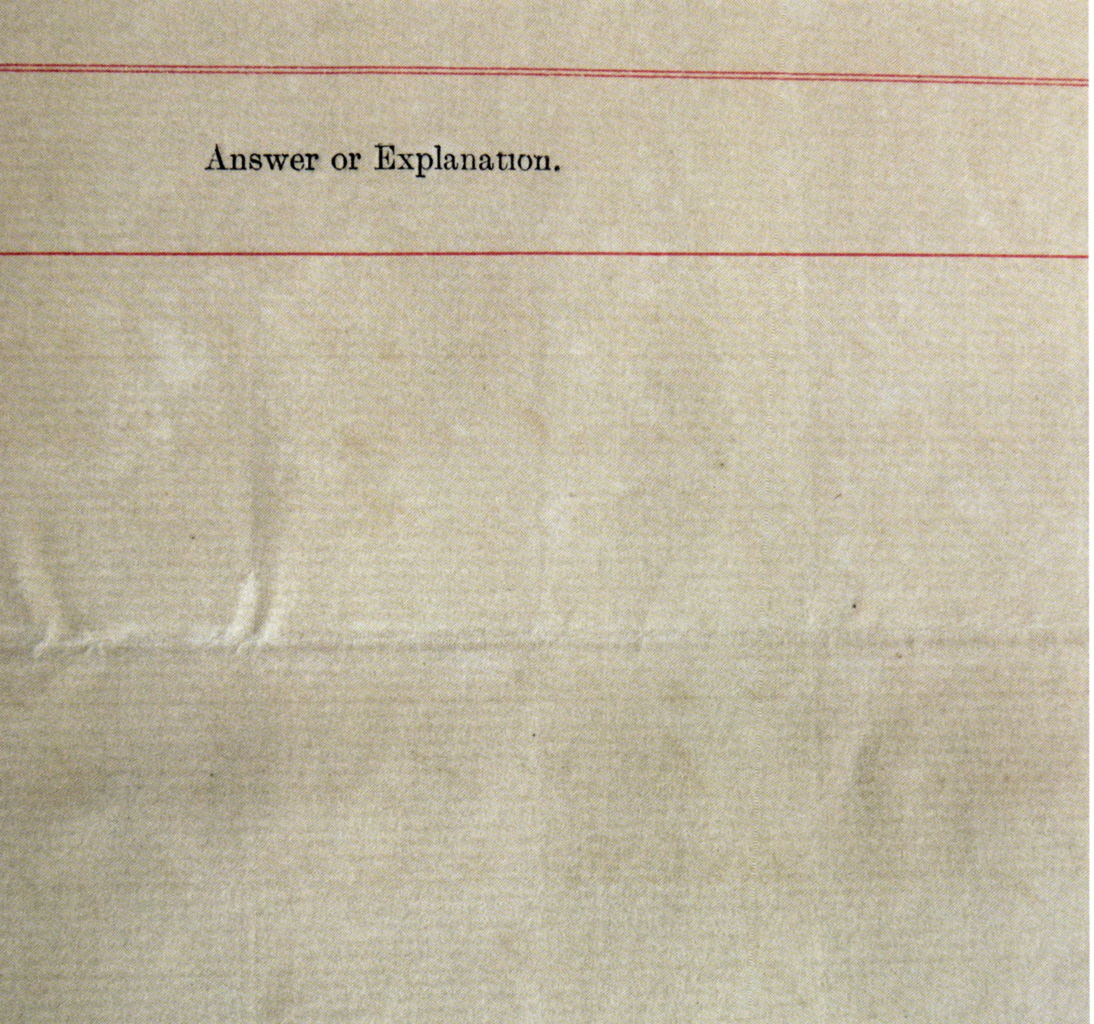
Answer or Explanation.

UGANDA

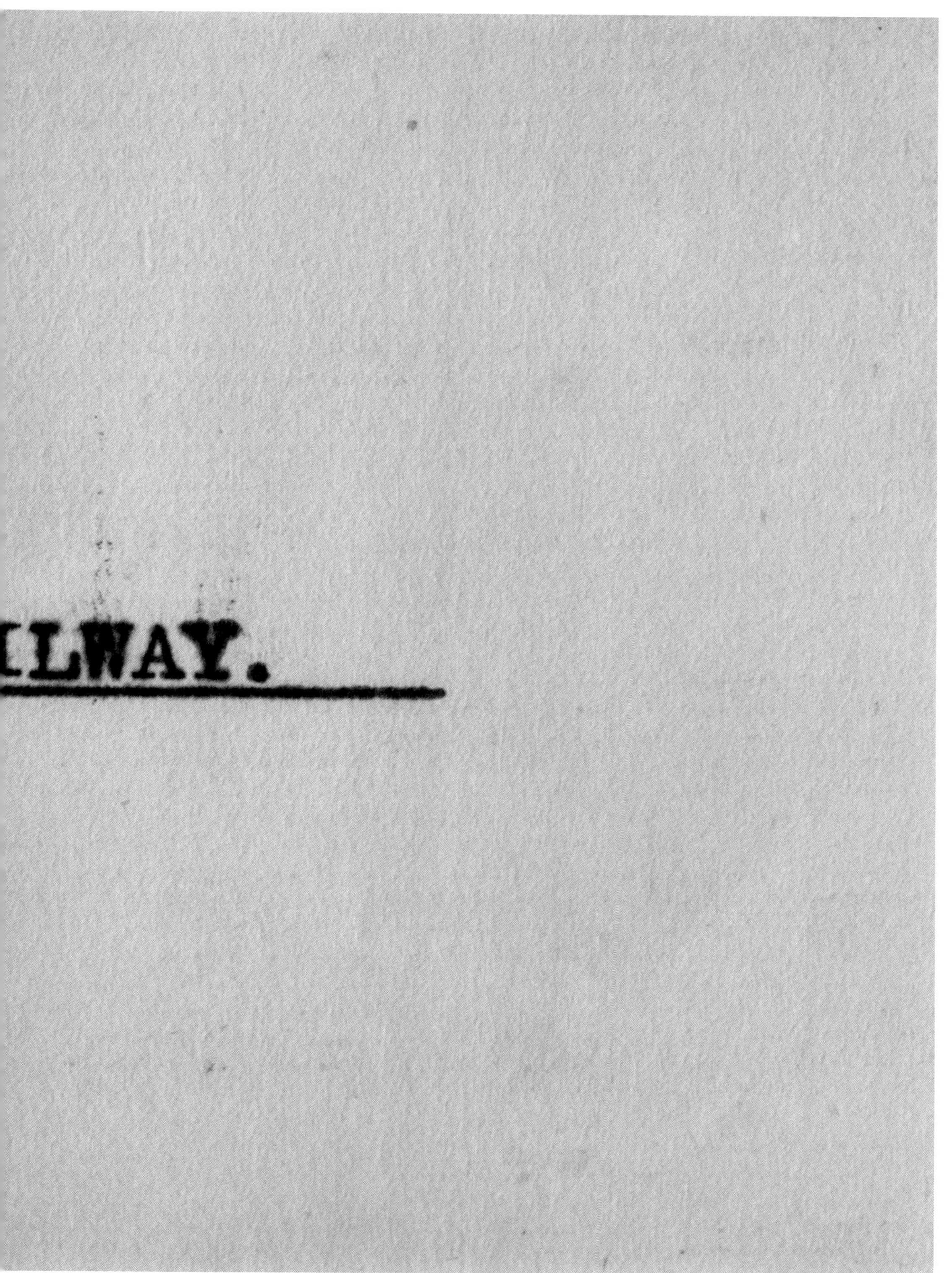
ILWAY.

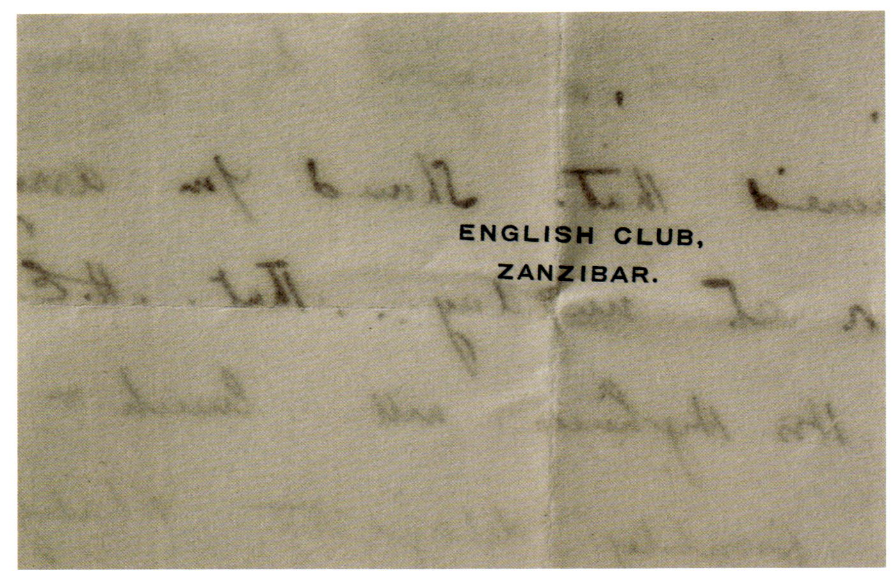

"While with   , he told a reporter,I had
seen all the horrors of the slave trade and the way in which
the slaves were hunted and driven to the coast.According to
the treaties existing at the time,the slave trade was
perfectly legal and we had no power to stop it. The slaves
were brought in to be employed in the cleve plantations and
to be smuggled to Persia,Arabia,Turkey and elsewhere. The
whole trade was in the hands of the Indians,who were British
subjects, but who preferred to be considered under Arab
protection,as they were well aware what British ideas were
on the subject of the slave trade.I saw that the only way of
getting rid of these men,who were the real power in the
country,under our authority,was to put an end to slavery!"
         ,therefore,induced the Sultan,by a purely
arbitrary act,to free the slaves." no compensation was paid

AFRICA. NO.3 1885

GENERAL ACT

OF THE

CONFERENCE OF BERLIN

SIGNED FEBRUARY 26, 1885

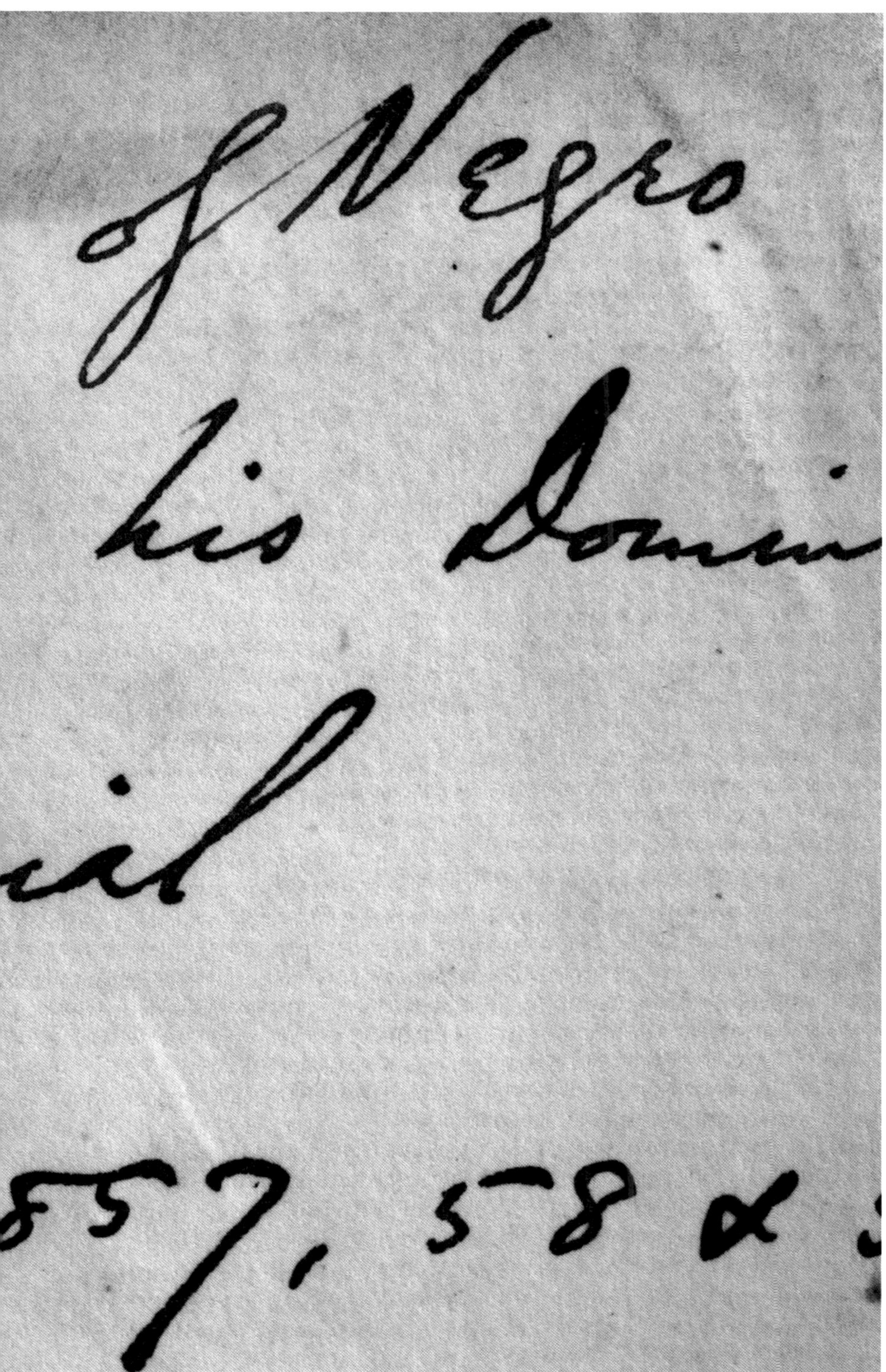

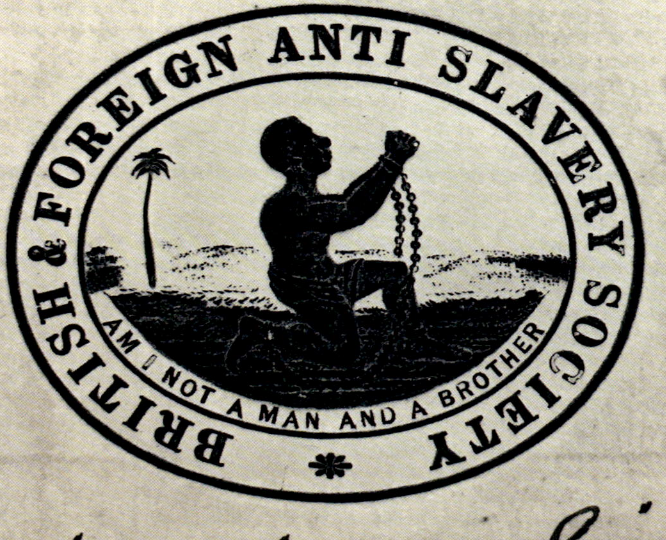

TELEGRAPHIC:
"UNYOKE LONDON."
British and Foreign
Copy
Private
BRITISH & FOREIGN ANTI SLAVERY SOCIETY
AM I NOT A MAN AND A BROTHER
My dear Sir

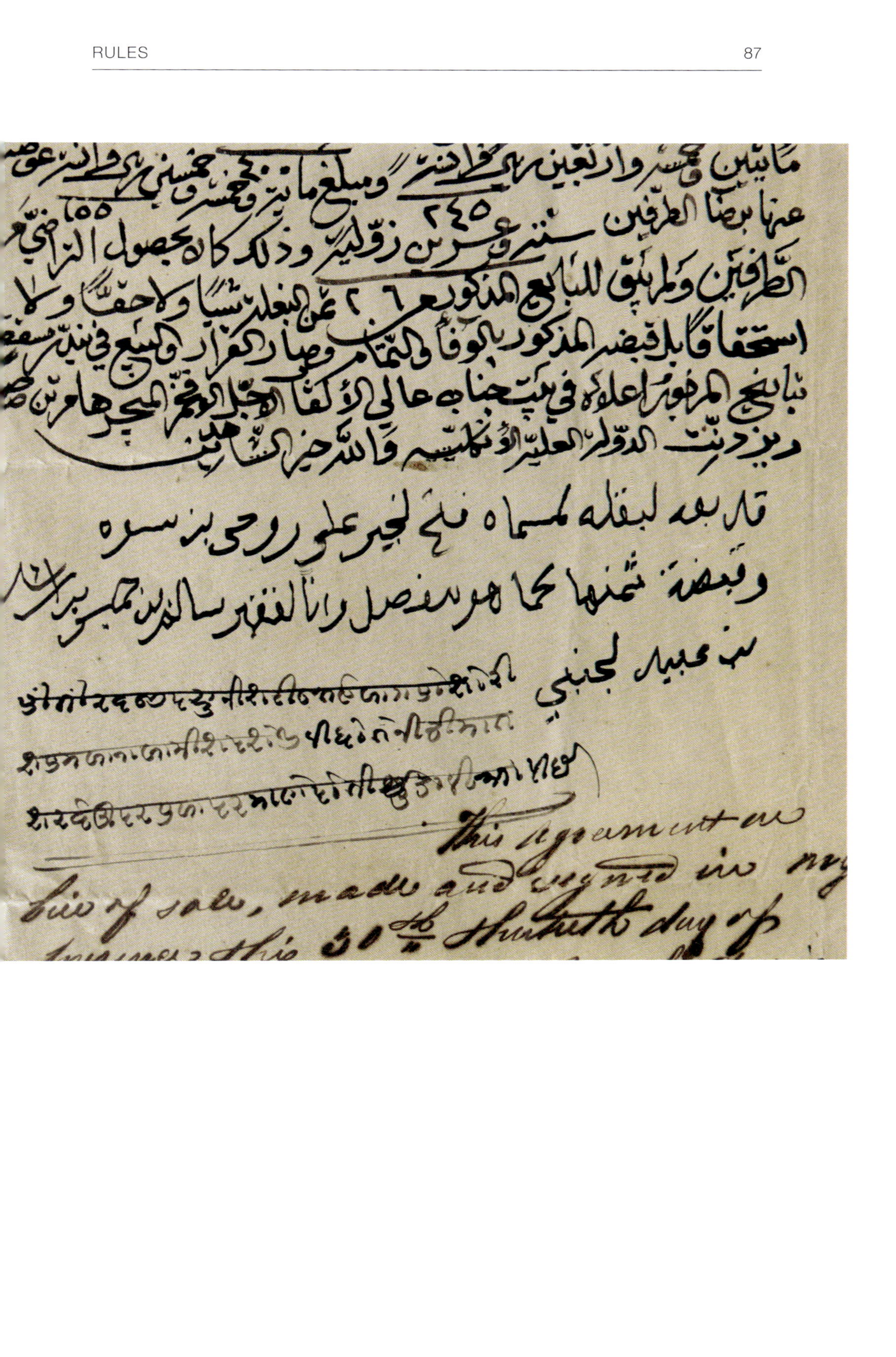

this agreement or bill of sale, made and signed in my ... business this 30th ... day of ...

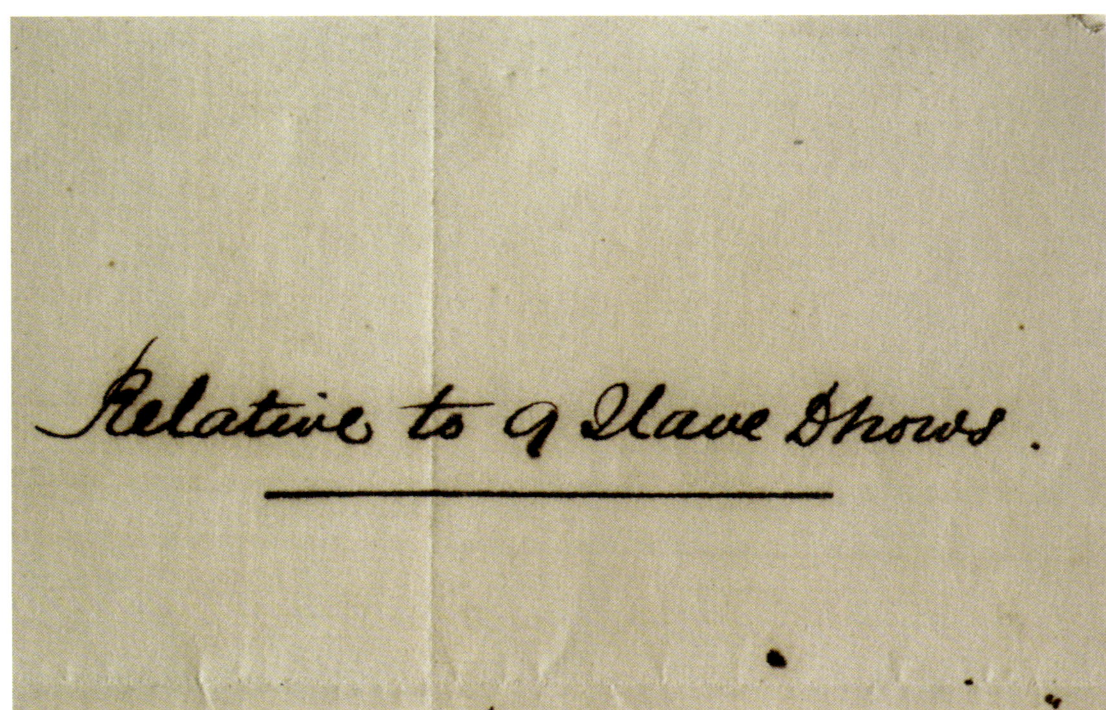

Relative to a Slave Shows

Calcutta, 31ˢᵗ March 1879

I have to acknowledge,

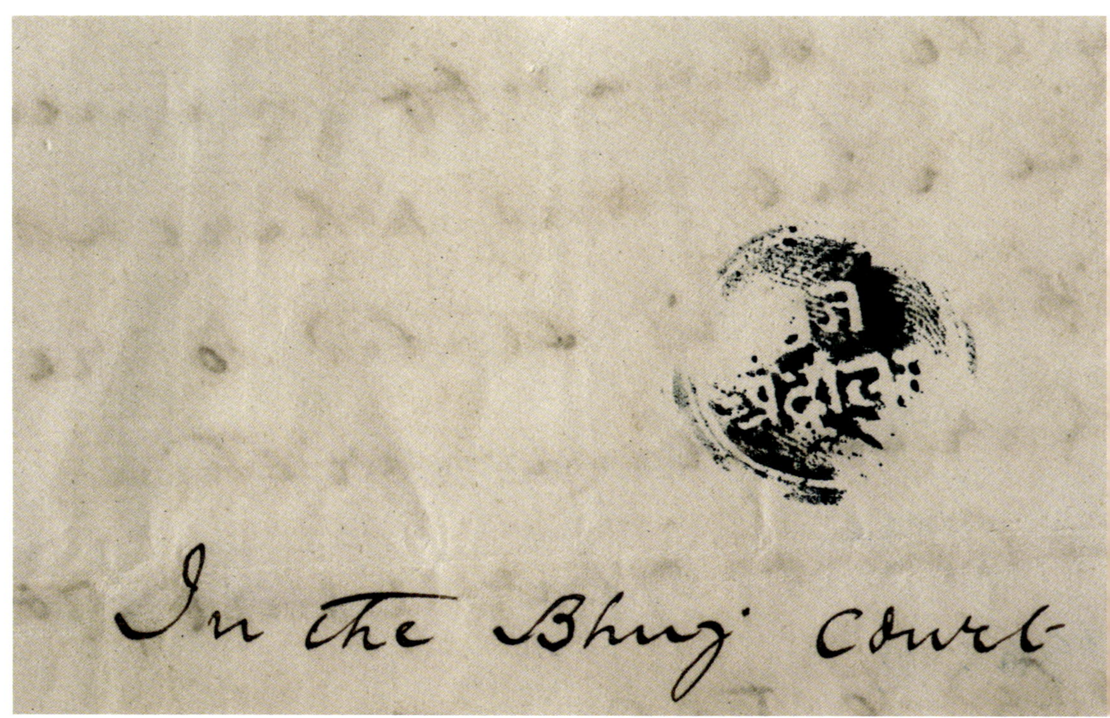

In the Bhuj court

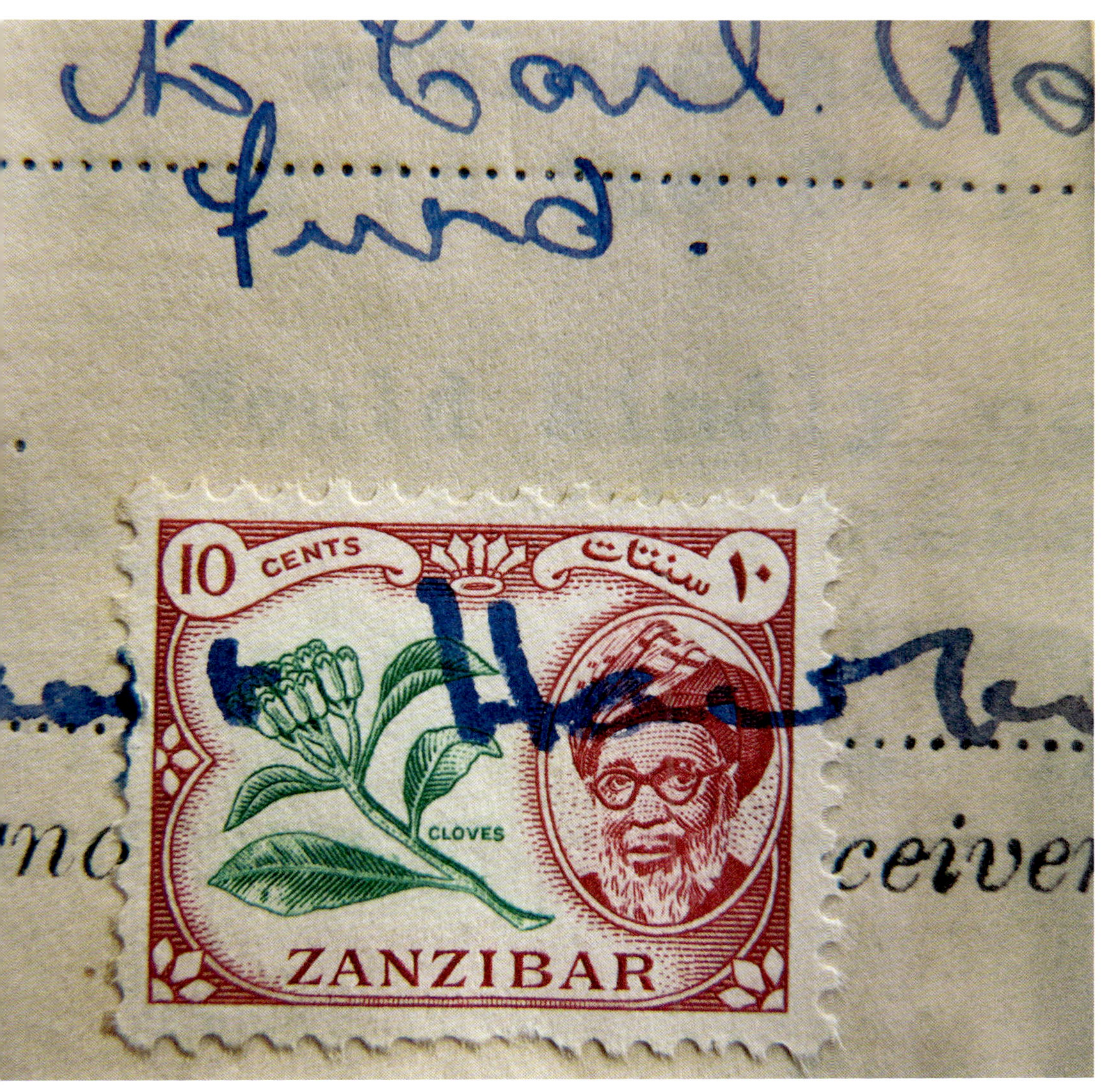

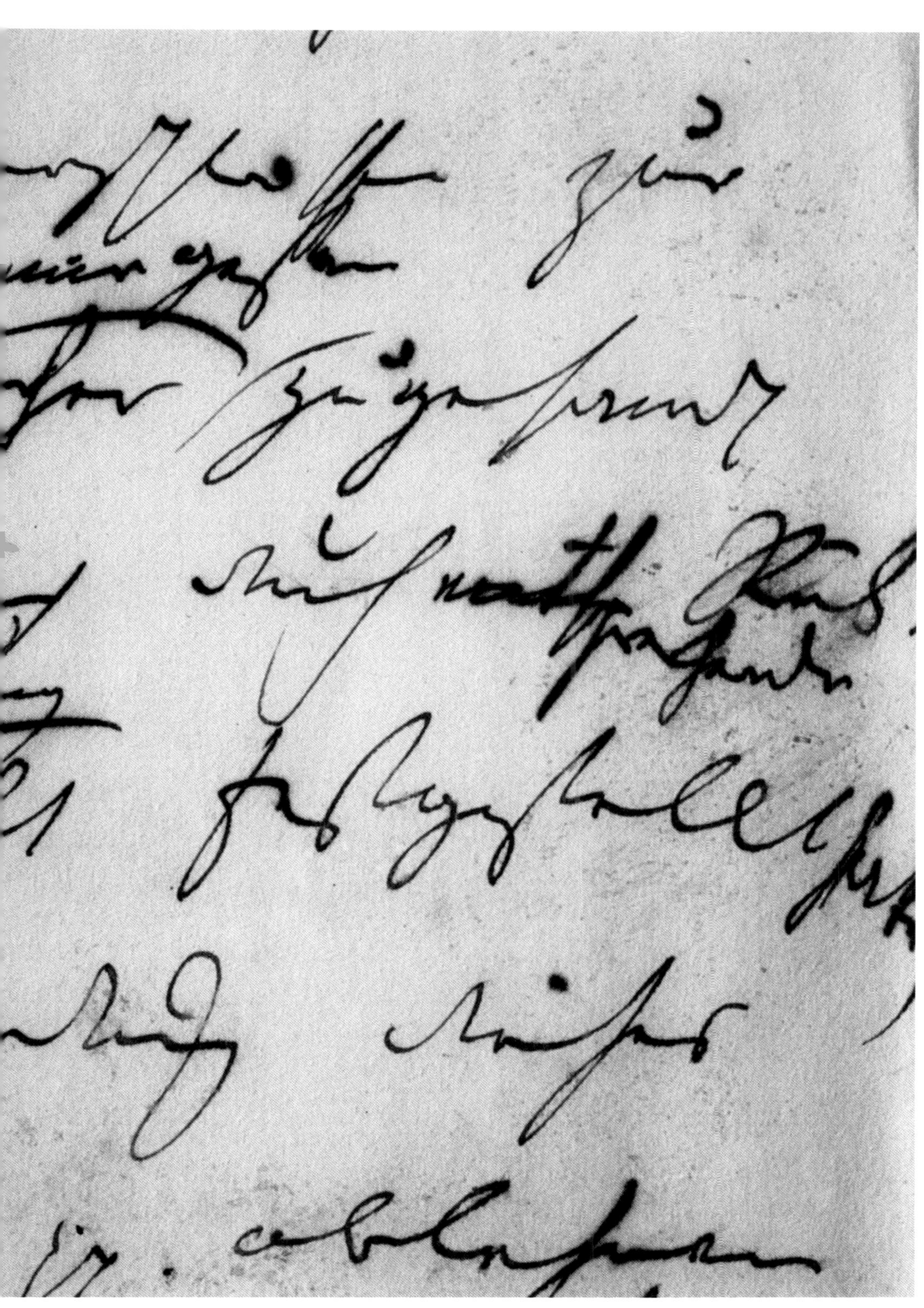

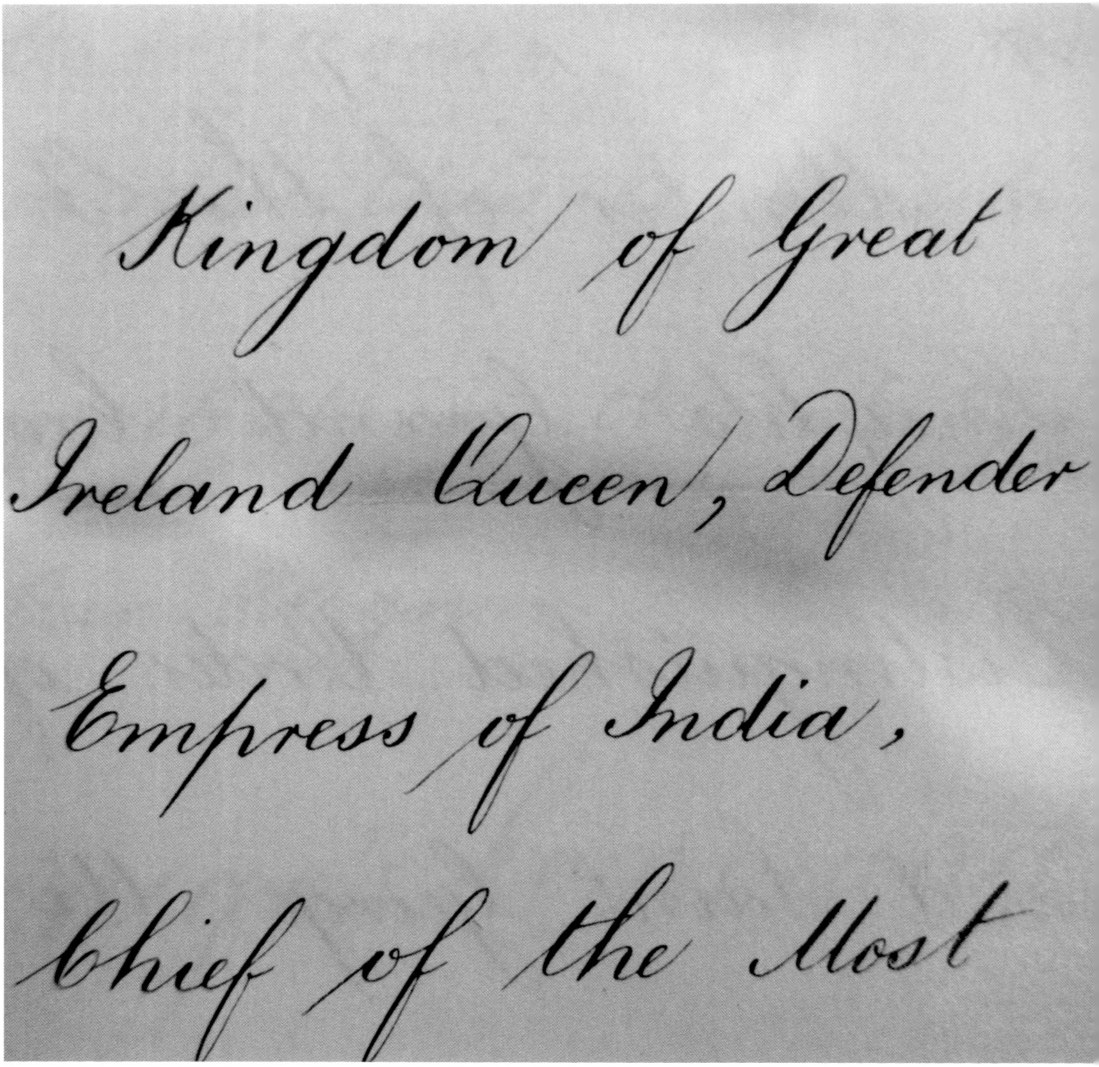

Kingdom of Great

Ireland Queen, Defender

Empress of India,

Chief of the Most

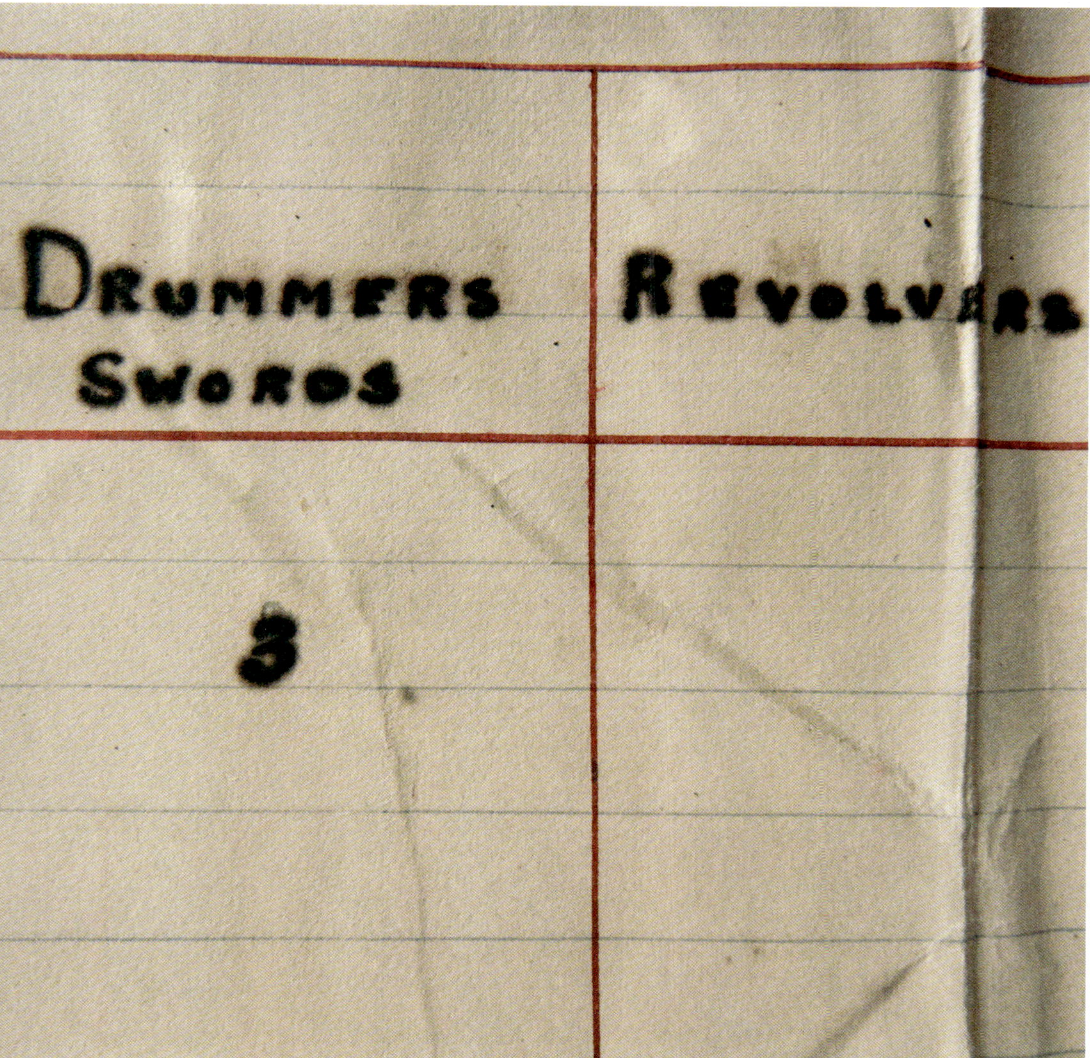
DRUMMERS REVOLVERS
SWORDS
3

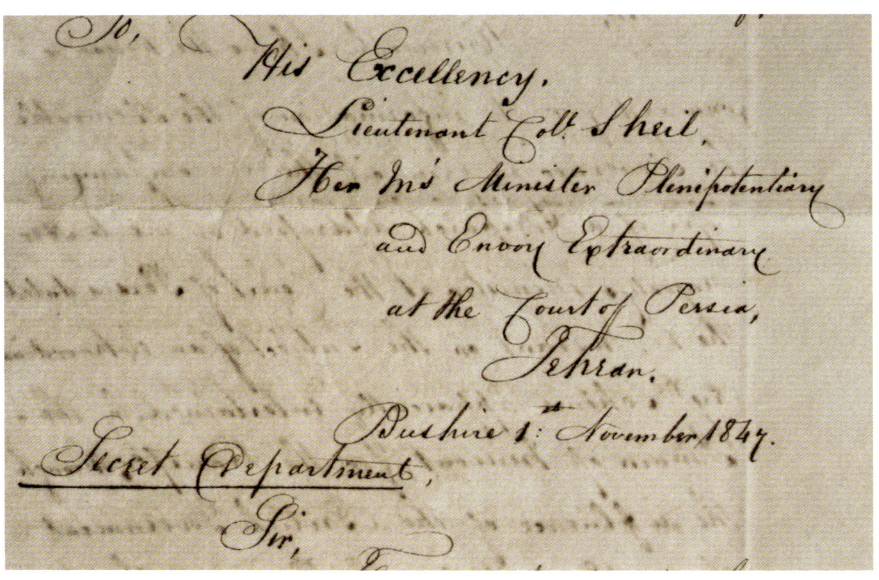

NATIVE AUTHORITY.   [CAP. **60**   585

CHAPTER 60.

Native Authority.

CAP. 60.

—

TO MAKE PROVISION FOR THE POWERS AND DUTIES NATIVE CHIEFS AND FOR THE INFORCEMENT OF NATIVE

Ordinance No. 17 of 1919.

A. Ord. 8 of 1921.

[28TH JUNE, 1919; 30TH JUNE, 1919.]

This Ordinance may be cited as the Native Authority   Short title.

... is not the man for such work and I hope if once your brother gets off on his Mission he will push straight on and give Sir   no chance of overtaking him. I am sure your brother will do the work far better than Sir   and I wish him to have the credit of it too.

Things are in a very unsatisfactory state between us and Germany as to African matters at present but I think we shall come out of the scramble not so badly if only our Government are firm.

Yrs vy sny

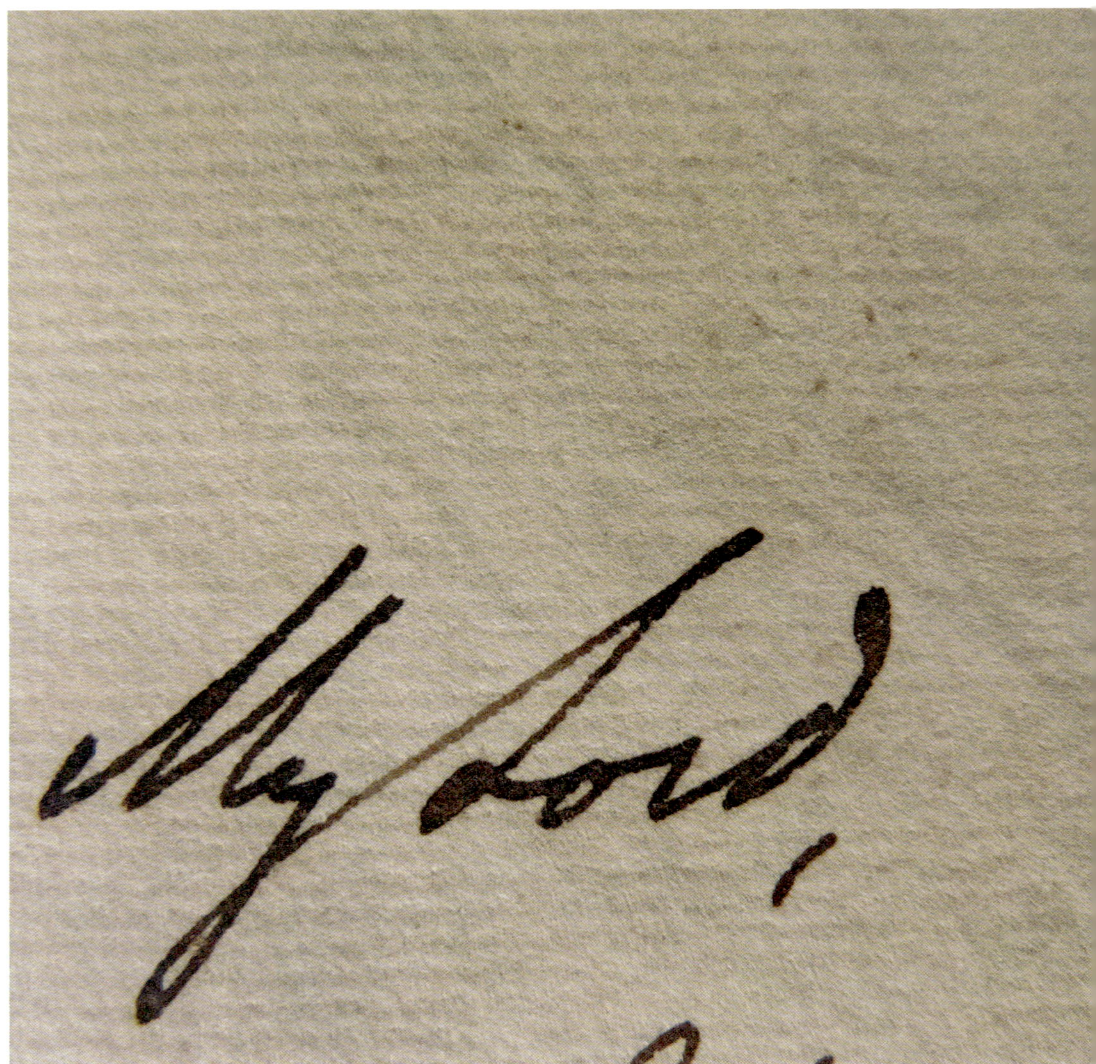

Imperial British East
Africa Company —
2 Pall Mall East

22 April 1890.

EUROPEAN STAFF

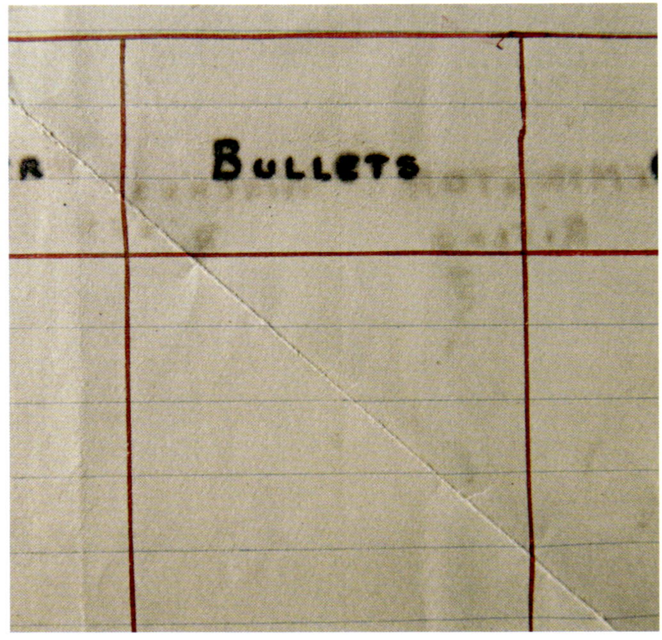

BULLETS

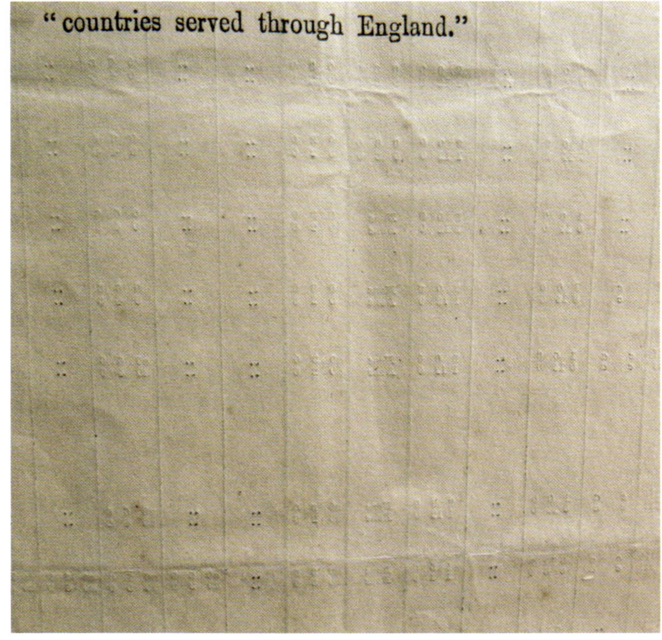

"countries served through England."

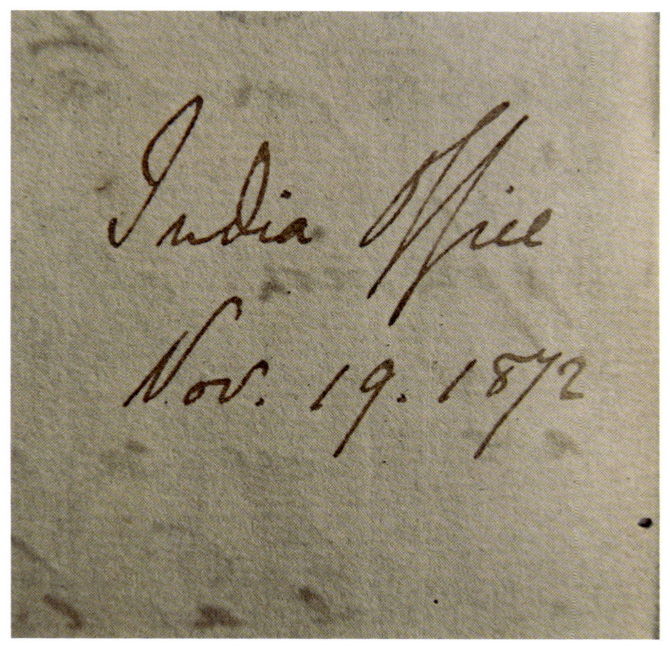

SUB-INSPECTORS

Fatima wanted to work with her camera. She wanted to use a macro lens. For her light is the subject matter, through colour, line, tone and composition. Beauty is powerful and it's not linear. She wanted to find the subtexts to the words 'East Africa Protectorate'. She was interested in details such as the embossing of the word '*Deutsches*', its colour, its texture, and how it reminded her of sounds and voices in Europe. She was in the world of 'God and my lawful right', '*Dieu et ma main droite*', '*Dieu et mon droit*'; with red ink 'KENYA', 'God and my right', '*Honi soit qui mal y pense*', 'May he be shamed who thinks badly of it', 'Shame be to him who thinks ill of it'. 'Protectorate' means a state that is controlled and protected by another. Fatima wanted to feel the fibres of the paper, the writing, the colour of the ink. She wanted to read the letters again and again. She wanted to feel the force with which it all happened. The purple ink was terrifying. It was like opening exam results. She could feel in her hands the power of an authority that could quite easily get rid of her and wipe away any evidence, an authority that could rewrite an event with a different account and she would just have to accept it. It was the terror of authority.

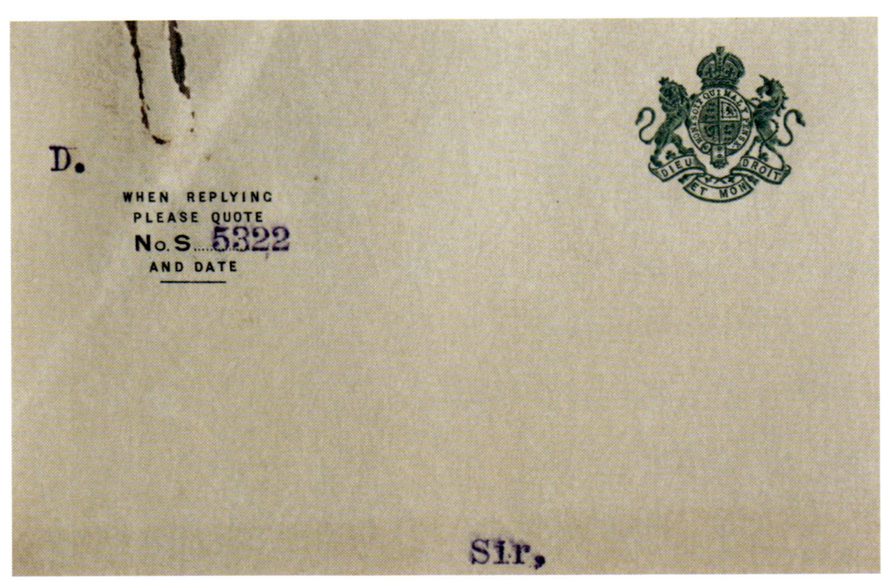
D.

WHEN REPLYING
PLEASE QUOTE
No. S. 5322
AND DATE

Sir,

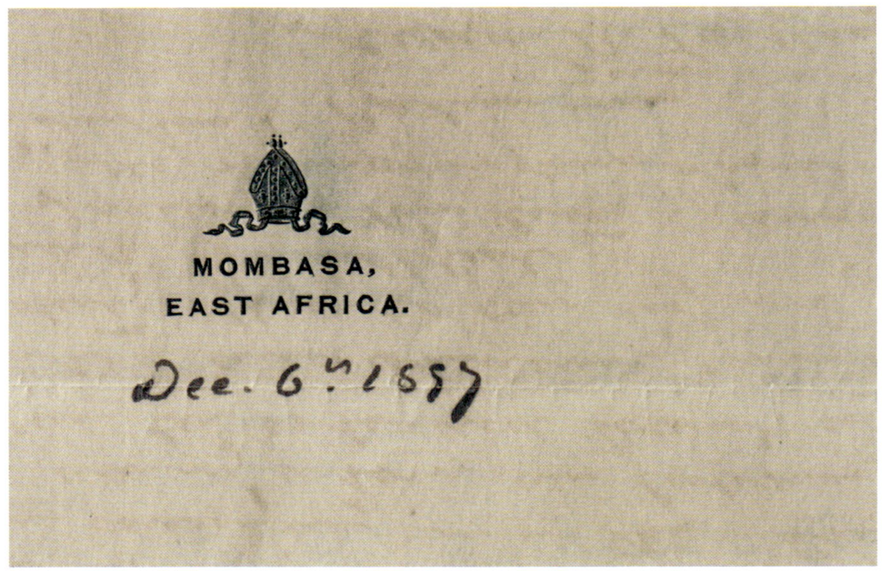
MOMBASA,
EAST AFRICA.

Dec. 6th 1857

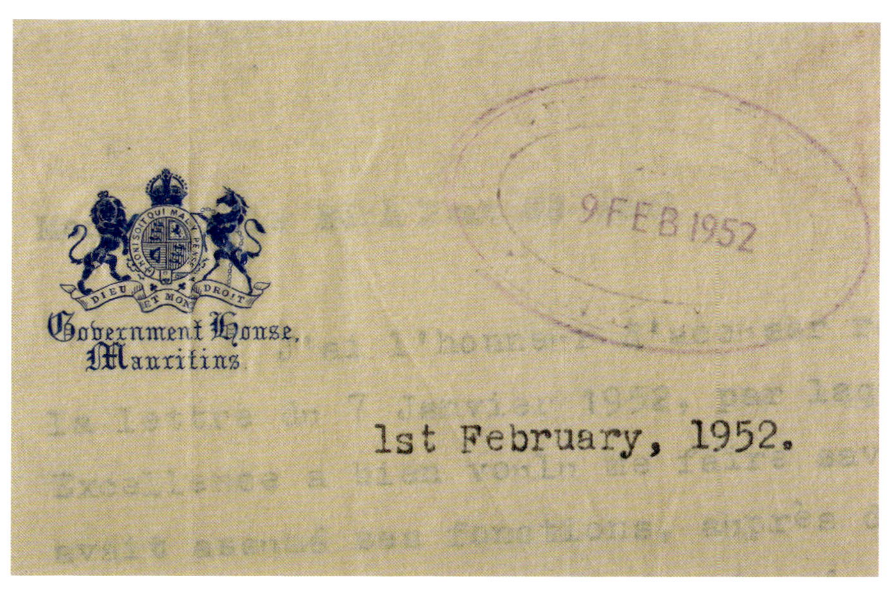

Government House,
Mauritius

1st February, 1952.

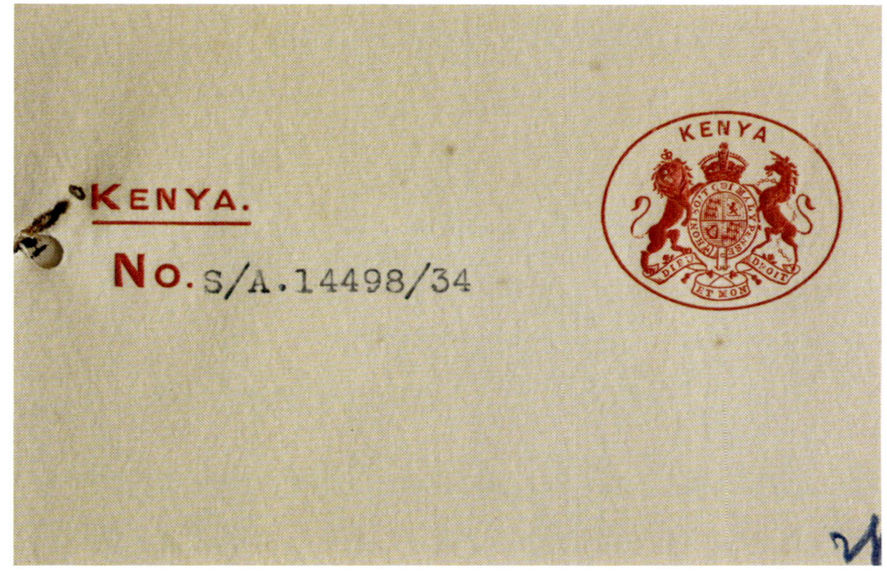

KENYA.

No. S/A.14498/34

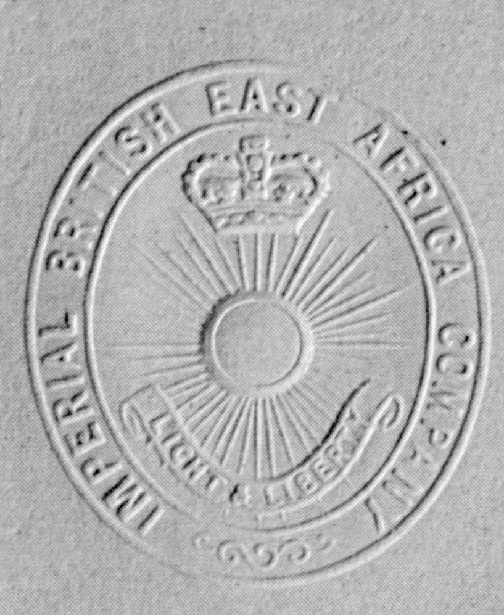

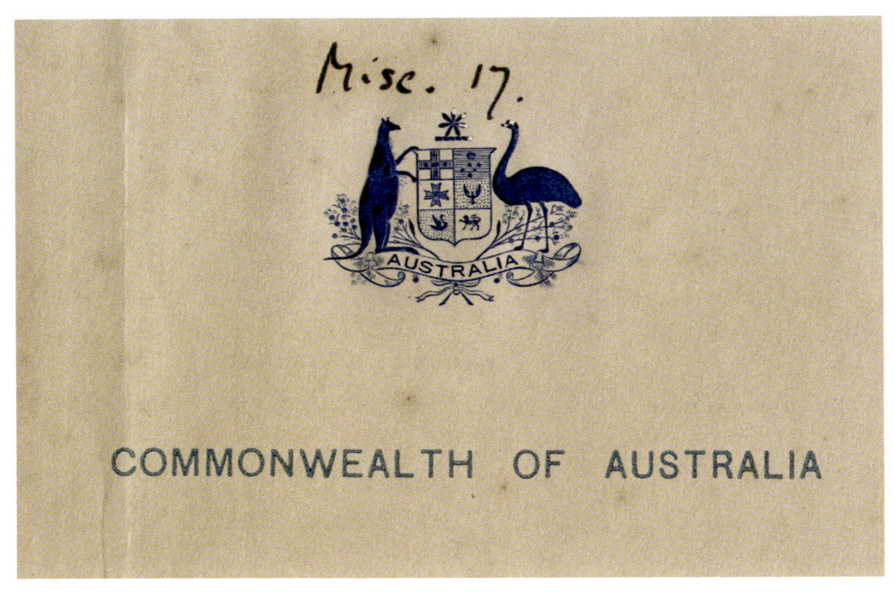

COMMONWEALTH OF AUSTRALIA

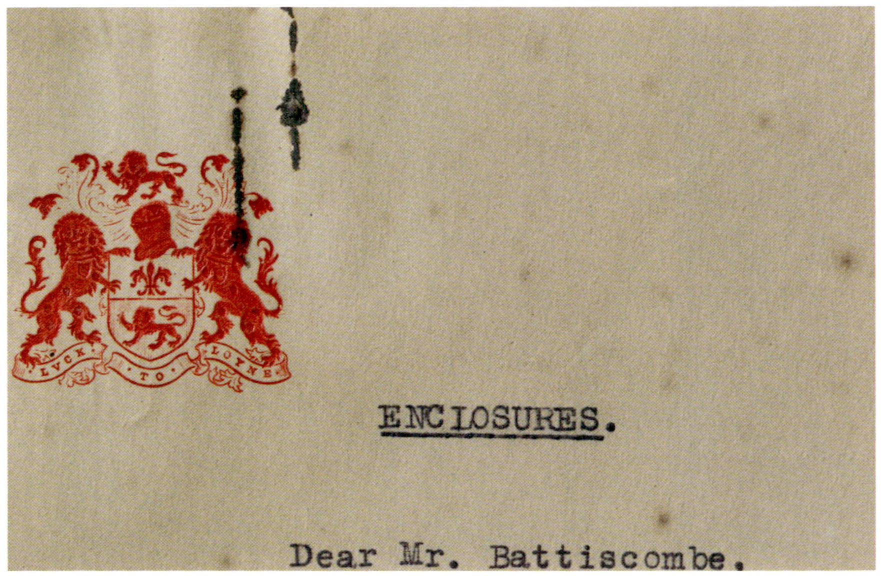

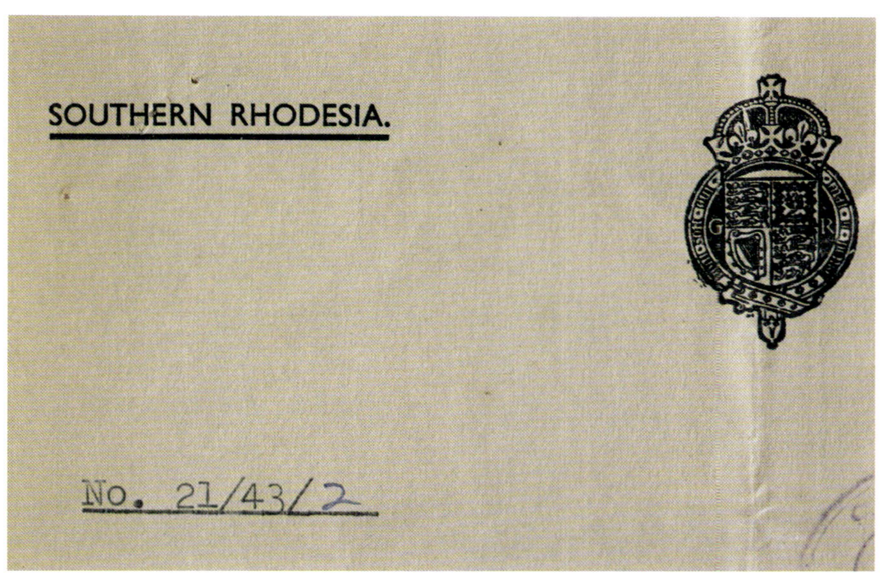
SOUTHERN RHODESIA.
No. 21/43/2

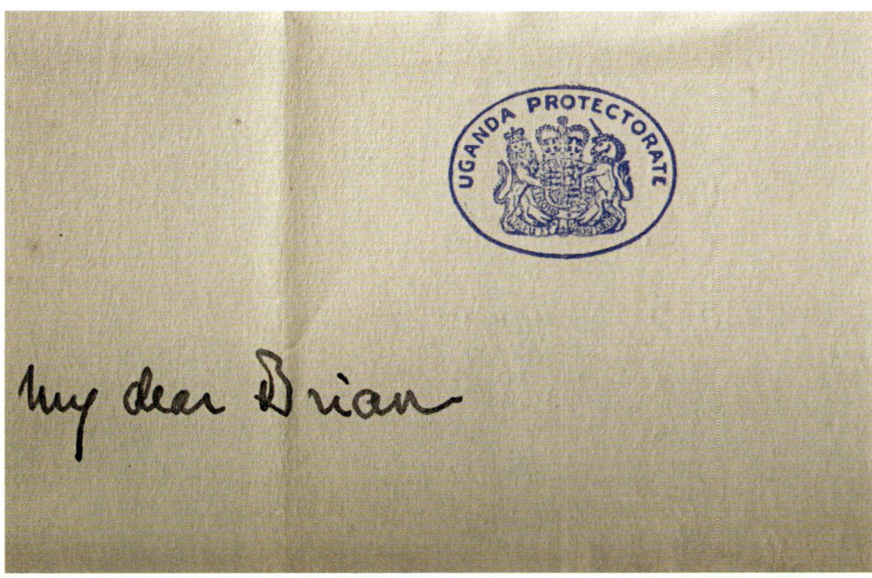
UGANDA PROTECTORATE
My dear Brian

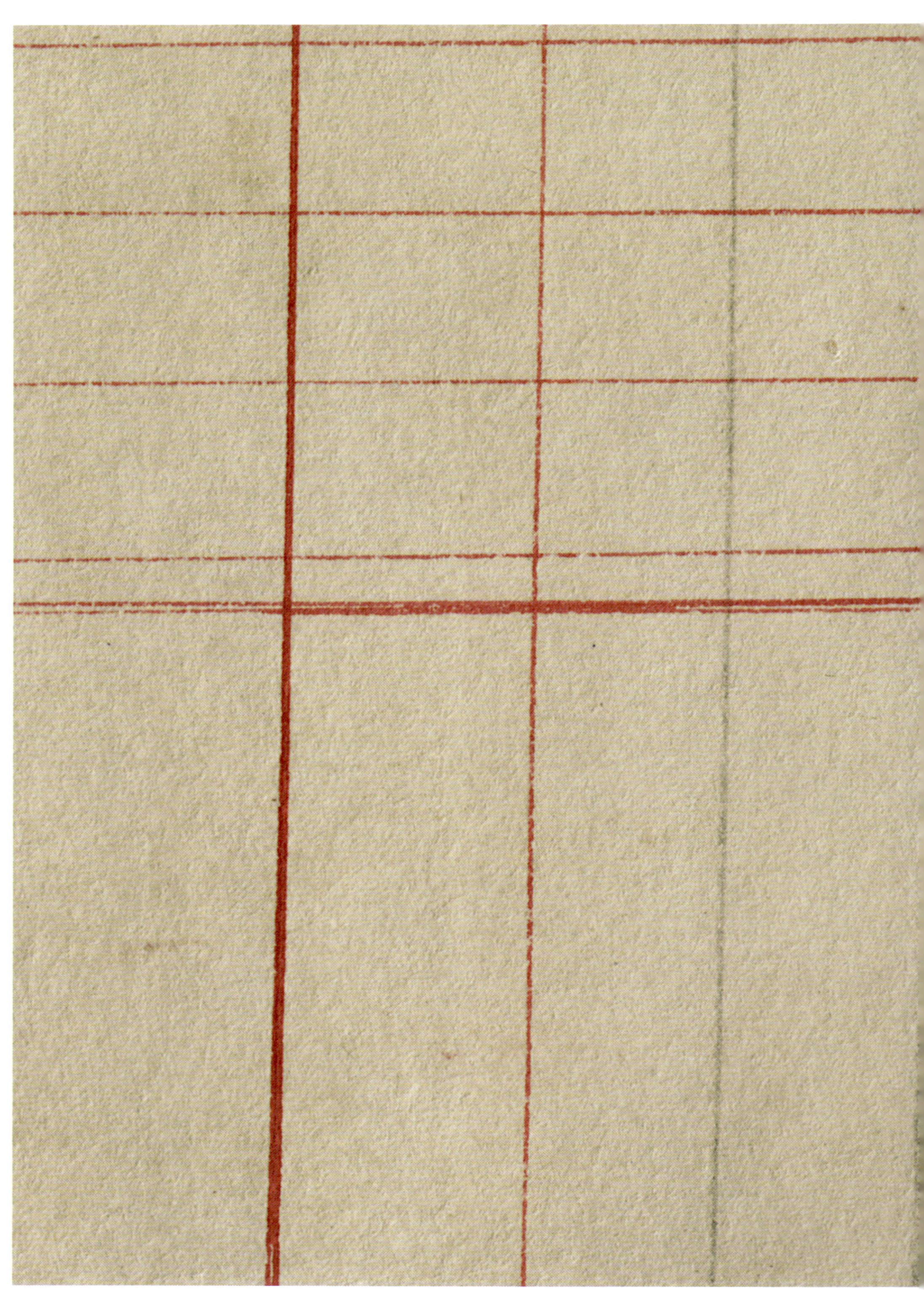

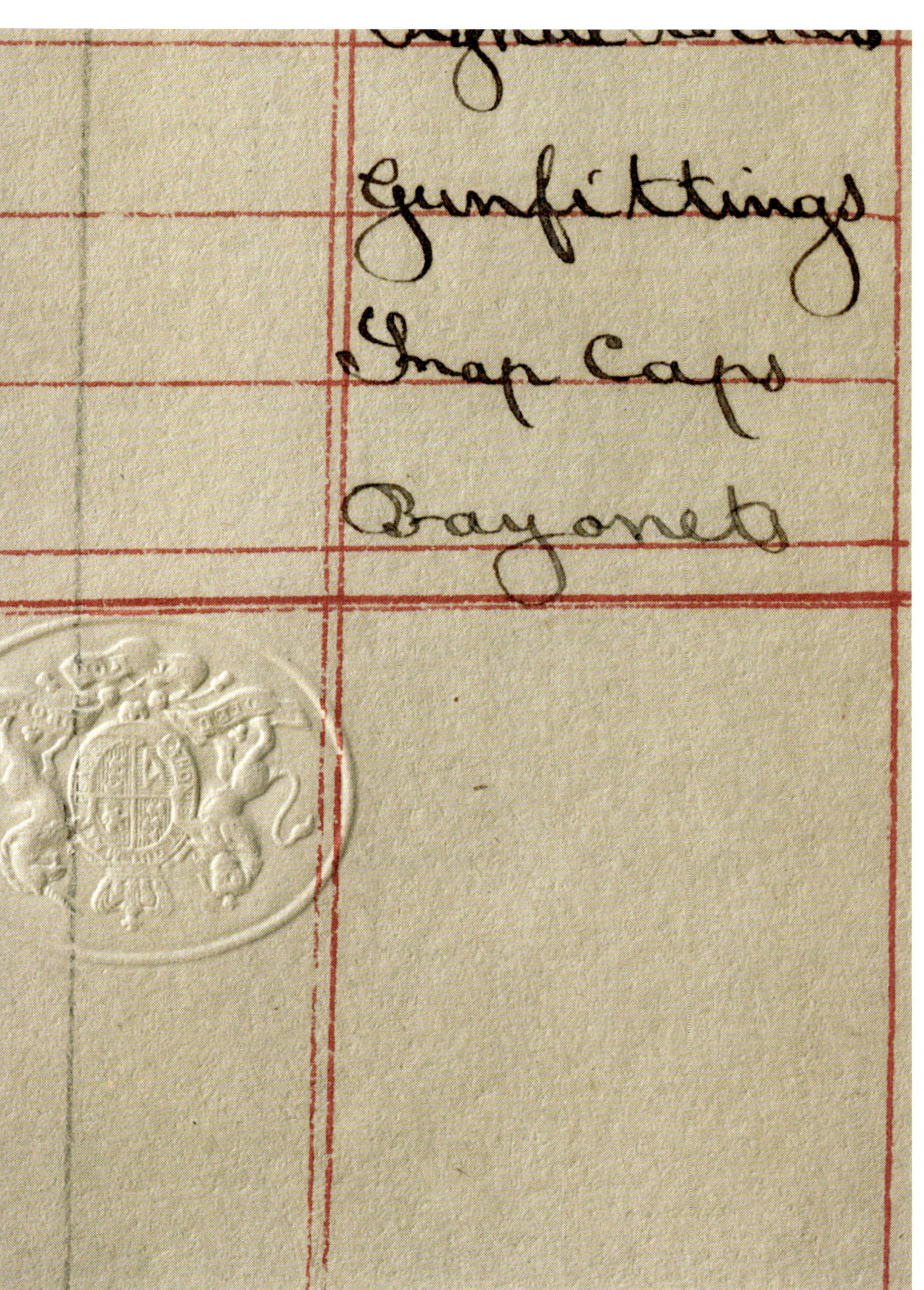
Gunfittings
Snap Caps
Bayonet

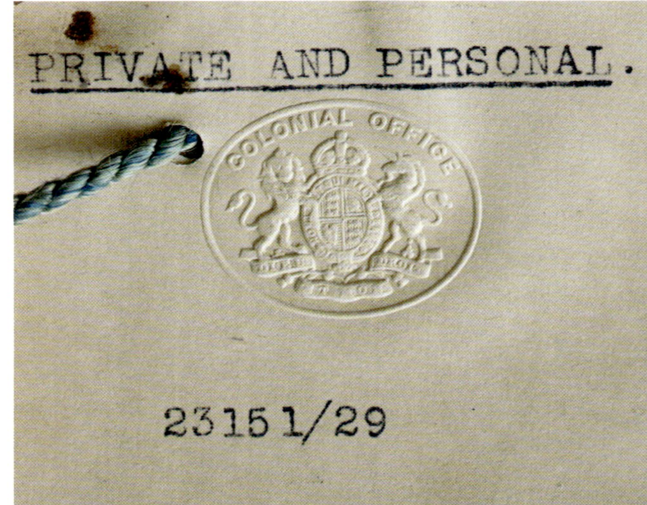

<u>PRIVATE AND PERSONAL</u>.

23151/29

My dear Battiscombe,

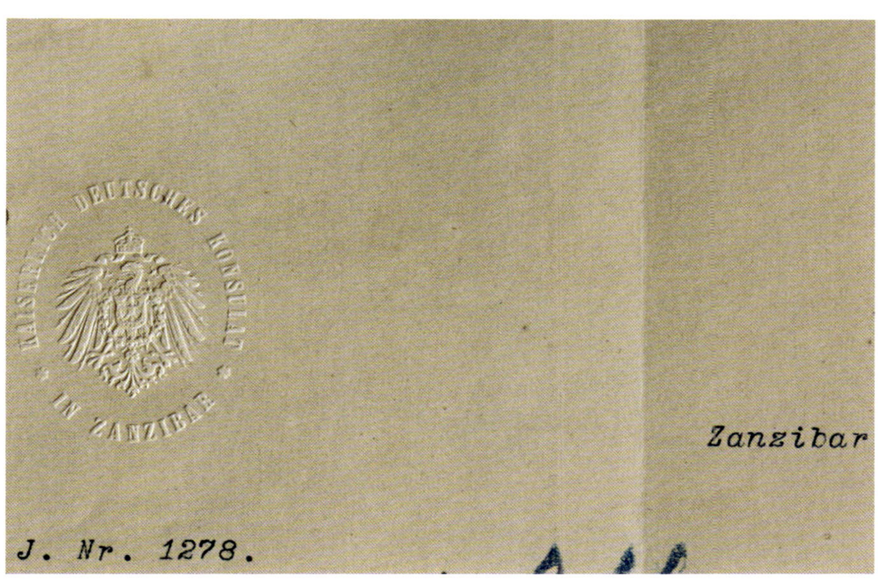
KAISERLICH DEUTSCHES KONSULAT IN ZANZIBAR
Zanzibar
J. Nr. 1278.

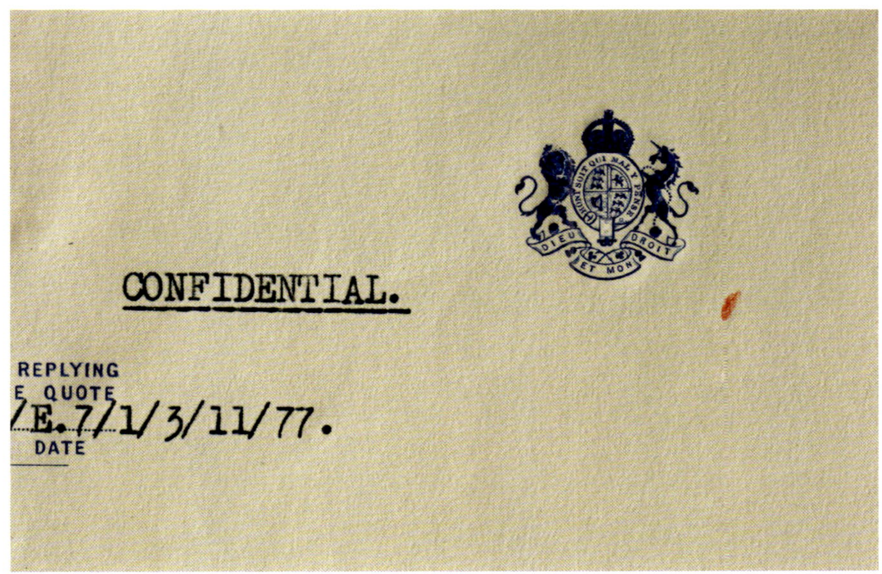
CONFIDENTIAL.
DIEU ET MON DROIT
HONI SOIT QUI MAL Y PENSE
REPLYING
E QUOTE
/E.7/1/3/11/77.
DATE

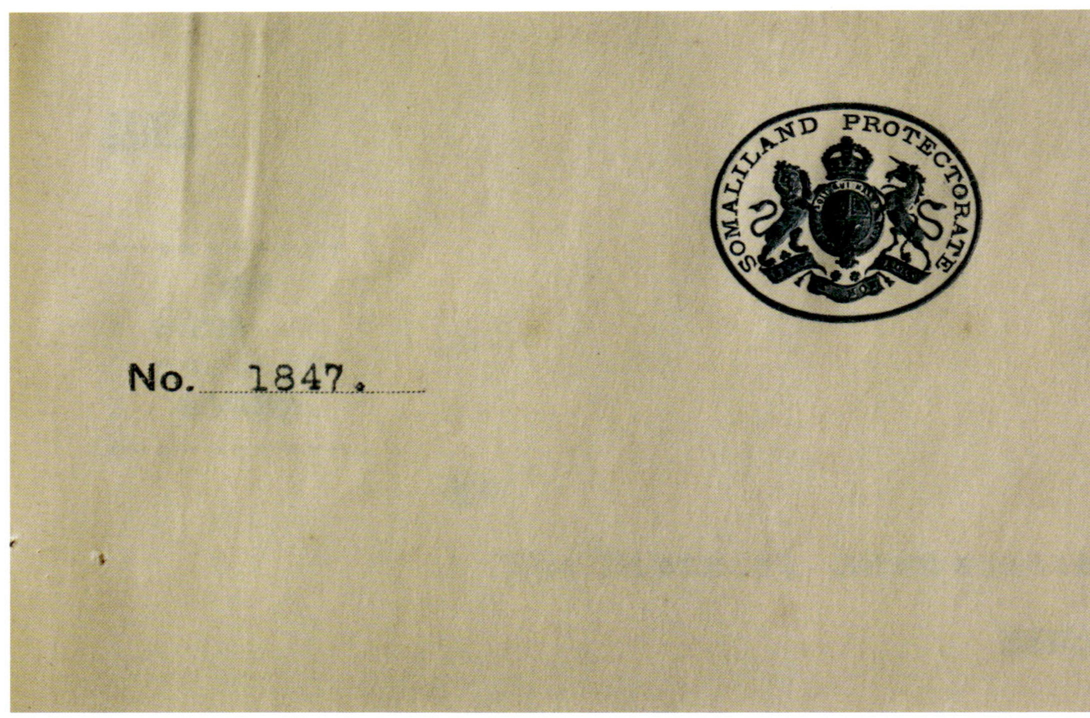

No.   1847.

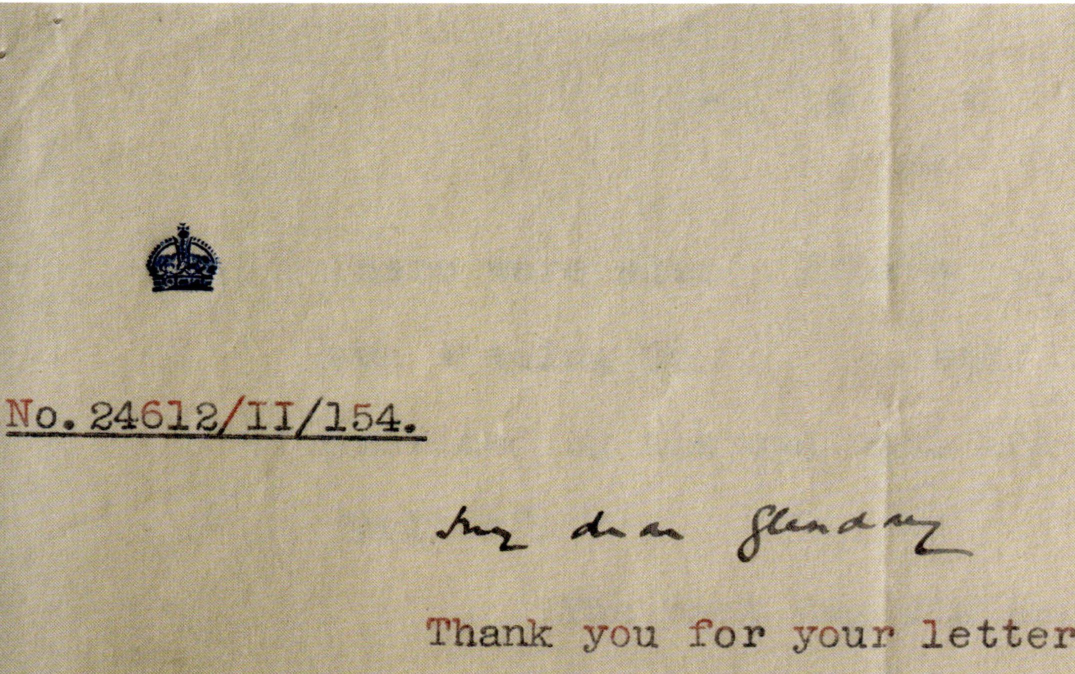

No. 24612/II/154.
My dear Glenday
Thank you for your letter

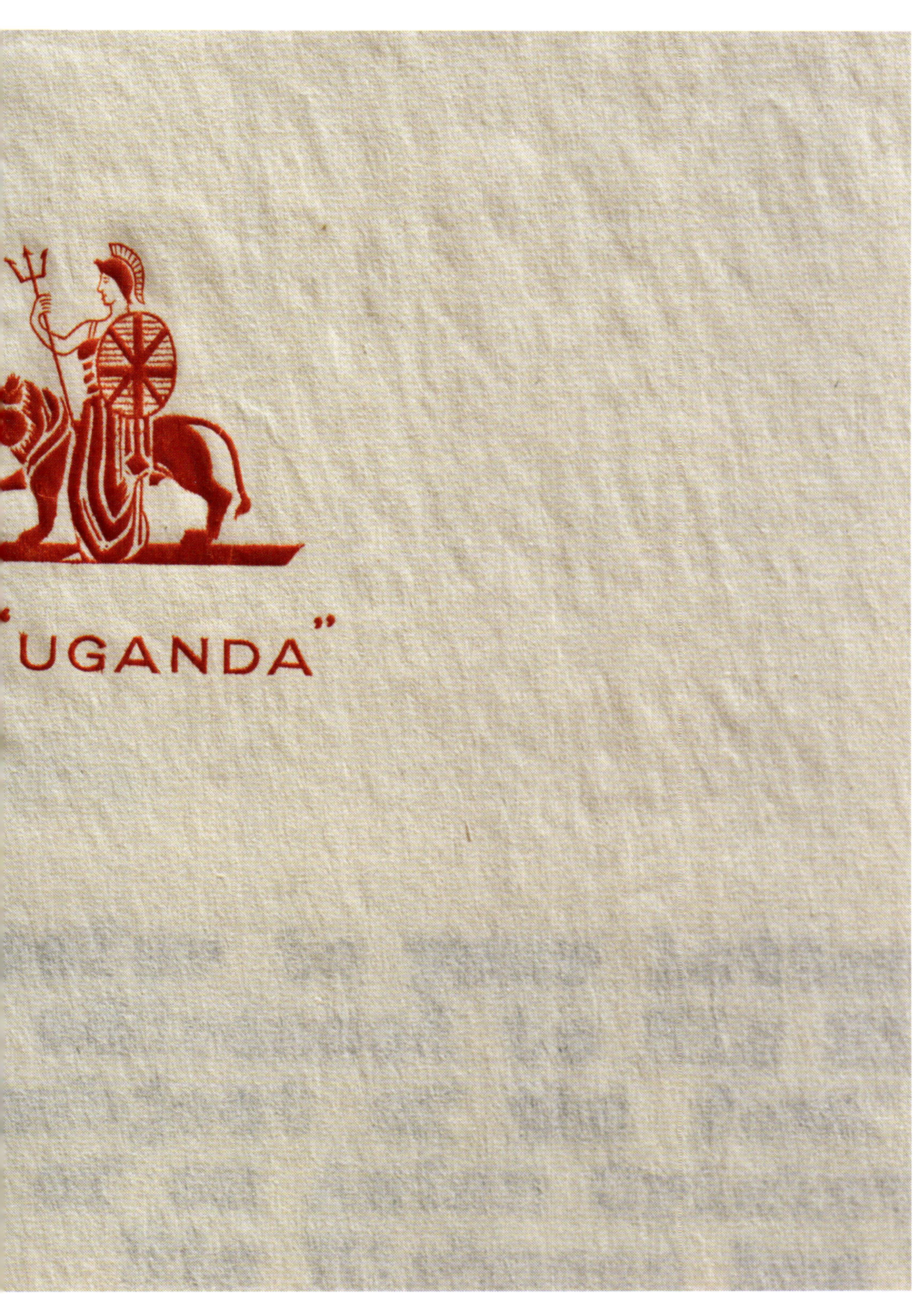
"UGANDA"

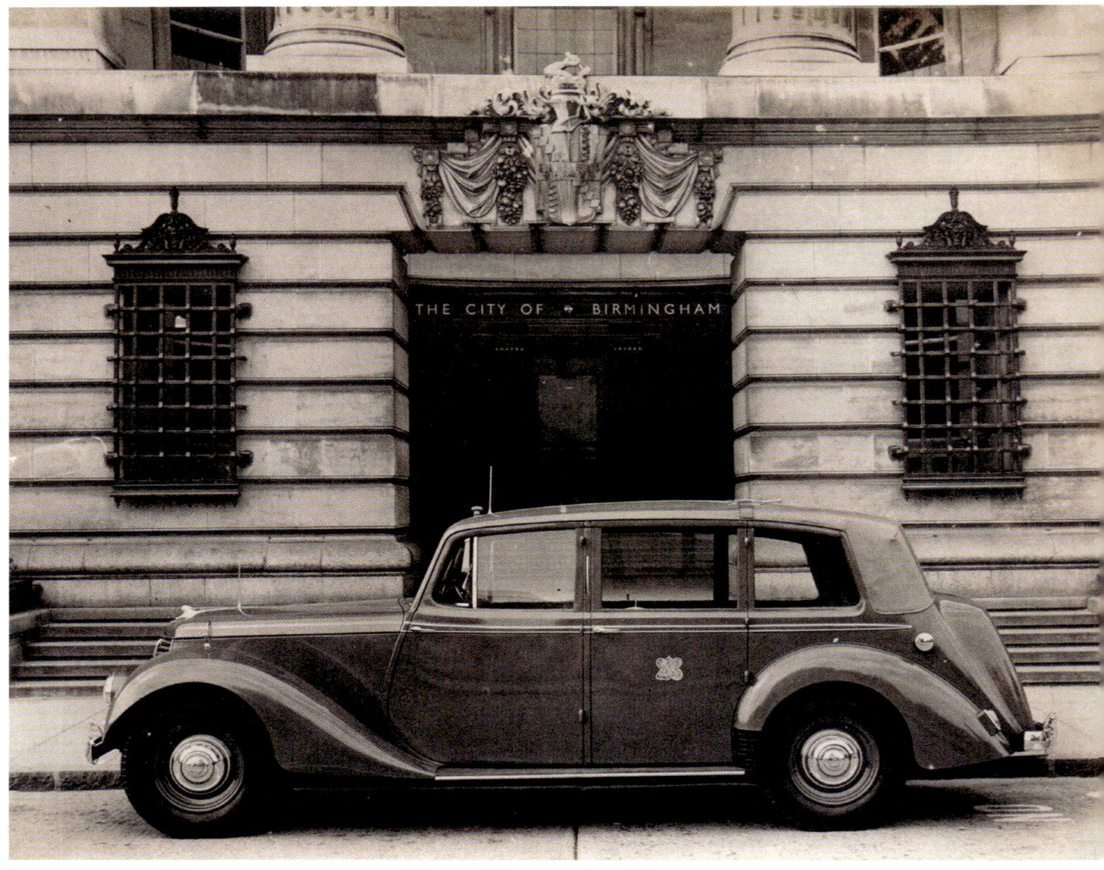
THE CITY OF · BIRMINGHAM

STAMPED ON THE BODY:
AESTHETICS OF POWER AND DECAY IN ZARINA BHIMJI'S *LEAD WHITE*
M. Neelika Jayawardane

In the installation *Lead White*, 2018, the artist Zarina Bhimji explores the minutiae left behind by violent upheavals and conquering armies. Her work – the result of years of research at the Zanzibar National Archives – asks us to consider the imprint of the legacies of the powerful and the monumental, through careful attention to the debris left behind by their institutions. As with her previous films, the images in this installation form a conceptual inquiry that remarks on the fluidity of memory and the seeming permanence of objects. As an investigation into light and colour, these images become 'vehicles for meditation on legality, power and beauty'.[1]

Bhimji notes that she begins her process as though she is at work on 'a crime novel or as an investigator arriving at the scene.'[2] However, she is not focussed on identifying 'the murderer or the victim';[3] rather, she is thinking about the social dynamics that produce such 'crimes', as well as the long aftermath of violence on those who inherit the effects of the crime. Her camera focusses on the ephemera carelessly left behind, containing echoes and whispers that allude to the mindset of perpetrators, the 'moral ambiguity' of those who masterminded the crime and 'the political and economic pressure [that] existed for them',[4] as well as the subsequent justifications for violent actions.

Architectural details of colonial structures, vehicles used by colonial and postcolonial officials and details of documents show up repeatedly. These architectural forms, memory-keepers of the footprints of intervention and occupation, allow Bhimji to meditate on the aesthetics of power and its twin nemeses: decay and forgetting. Despite her obvious preoccupation with spaces carrying potent narratives, political power and memory, she stresses that her work is also concerned, instinctively, with aesthetics, emphasising, 'I'm interested in colour. I'm not only interested in the political – I'm interested in texture. Beauty is important and political … to reclaim beauty is about reclaiming dignity. I want the work to be "quieter" – because then the beauty can be foregrounded; it can be tender.'[5]

As observers, we realise that whilst the grand architectures and material cultures on which the empires built themselves remain, all their glory has now been left to dissipate into dust. It is also clear that the bits of paper to which Bhimji draws attention –

marked with ink, abstract fragments of handwritten script, sections of typewritten words and stamped imprints – are repositories of the precision with which power acts. These are orders, conveyed down lines of command, the end result of which was violence on far-away bodies and communities. The discarded ephemera and records on paper are also silent receptacles embodying power and desire. They speak as voluminously as witnesses would. It is these fragments of paper – used for centuries to intimidate and subjugate, to transfix the colonial subject as an object, and to make this object's desire for mobility and subjectivity a beggar's task – that give away the secrets of empire.

Imprint and Aesthetics of Power

Bhimji's work has always drawn our attention to the deep imprint – on land, objects and bodies – resulting from drastic shifts in systems of rule. In the introductory texts to her 2013 exhibition at the Whitechapel Gallery, Bhimji specifies that 'My work is not about the actual facts but about the echo they create, the marks, the gestures and the sound. This is what excites me.' As with her previous film and photographic installations, the images included in *Lead White* follow narrative threads and the 'echo' created by monumental events. In *Lead White*, her photographs gesture towards an incomplete archive: the bureaucrat's wooden desk and cubicle, the debris of those who used marble, high-ceilinged buildings and crystal chandeliers to convey their supremacy. By focussing on discarded minutiae and the silences they carry, she finds a location in which to think. Ultimately, she says she is drawn to this material because it provides her with ways to 'make a visual language … between the political and poetic'.[6] In this way, she shifts our focus from the grand narratives of history, the achievements through which national identities and the majesty of rulers are composed towards individual experiences of the political.

It was important to go to the Zanzibar National Archives, Bhimji says, because it contains 'first-hand records of the British administration on the island'.[7] She also visited the House of Wonders (Beit al-Ajaib), which today is home to the Museum of History and Culture of Zanzibar and the Swahili Coast. Working on location, with first-hand records, 'enabled me to test out ideas … it's like being in a laboratory', where one can 'touch, feel and smell … the elements of force',[8] she notes. She remembers that she kept noticing how 'different forms of force kept coming in the documents'; conversely, when she was 'photographing objects, they kept expressing different forms of vulnerability'.[9]

The details on which her camera focusses draw our attention to networks of authority orchestrated by Britain, between itself and its colonies in East Africa and South Asia; she is careful to note, however, that she is interested in 'universal questions of power and inequalities that exist at the micro level',[10] and not just in the impact of Britain on Africa or Asia. Whilst the objects in the photographs may signal the ways in which empire and colonialism expressed itself, she insists that her work does not stop its investigation at colonialism alone. Thus, we see image after image of mundane, ordinary and once-beloved things, evidencing the ways that the day-to-day administration of power and its expression were made possible.

Fragments: Paper, Seals, Handwriting

The fragments of text and texture of paper contained in Bhimji's photographs communicate the ways in which the mechanisms of domination – necessary for an occupying force – remain powerful, long after the departure of the officers who carried out the duties of embodying and representing a distant and mighty ruler. These mechanisms remain as material realities in our institutional structures and, symbolically, in our still-colonised minds. Examining the minutiae is, perhaps, the only way to dissipate the power they continue to wield; we give ourselves time to meditate on the details that went into manufacturing the spectacle of majesty and the ability of empire to withstand decay. We comprehend what it took to maintain a seamless wall of power, by quelling opposition and pushing the boundary of one's entitlement ever further.

Even if we do not have a grounding in the specific historical events of the location from which these objects were retrieved, Bhimji's camera conveys the heft of history contained within these fragments of paper. Her photographs, focussing closely on details – a typewritten document, flowing handwriting in black India ink or a thread used to close an envelope – reflect on the relationship between the state and the individual. The calligraphy of a handwritten note, an ochre-red stamp on an official document and the yellowing paper itself, are also portals into less obvious meditations on colour, form and flow. This is the residue of a history so monumental that it impacted itself on entire geographical regions and signalled the displacement and removal of millions. Though they may be yellowing and desiccating, these bits of paper with their embossed seals continue to have remarkable staying power. The accounts they keep, down to shillings and cents, were no doubt the pride of some bureaucrat. The 'Protectorate of Zanzibar' and 'East Africa Protectorate' tell us of the arrival of British authority over the landscape, whilst the enduring Arabic calligraphy – on a letter addressed to a 'Mrs. Marshall-May' – is a reminder of a co-existing past.

Perhaps the most significant seal, or imprint, is that labelled 'AFRICA No. 3. 1886', which reads 'GENERAL ACT OF THE CONFERENCE OF BERLIN SIGNED FEBRUARY 26 1886'. This, along with a plethora of postage stamps with the names of various colonial protectorates and colonies, from Angola to Zanzibar, seems to be one of the most palpable, and seemingly benign remnants of the Berlin Conference. All of it, Bhimji says, is part of the original records of the Berlin Conference, maintained in the Zanzibar National Archives. She notes that the proceedings of the Conference not only had permanent effects on the continent of Africa as a whole – and to Europe – but also the particularities of day-to-day life in East Africa. The Berlin Conference, she points out,

> ... was unusual because international conferences were usually held to sort out the aftermath of a war, but almost never to settle problems before they led to war. The Congress spelled out the boundaries of the German claims in Africa (mostly at the expense of the Sultan of Zanzibar) and confirmed Germany as a major player in international affairs. In particular, the Congress accepted Bismarck's declaration of a protectorate over the East African territory mentioned in Karl Peter's treaties. A year later, the Anglo-German Treaty of 1886 ratified the protectorate by dividing Kenya (British) from Tanganyika (German) and allowing Zanzibar to remain independent and in control of a ten-mile deep coastal strip.[11]

Another seal, depicting the coat of arms of Lancaster is addressed to a 'Mr. Battiscombe'. This is possibly the same Mr Edward Battiscombe who was Acting Conservator of Forests in East Africa during the first decade of the twentieth century, known for creating a catalogue of *Trees and Shrubs of Kenya Colony*, which sold for five shillings.[12] Seals from India and Bombay, and letters written in Gujarati's distinctive *abugida* or alphasyllabary – a segmental writing system in which units of consonant-vowel sequences, based on a consonant base letter and added notations to denote vowels – relay the triangulated relationship created between Britain's crown jewels in East Africa and South Asia. There is little here, in this collection, to speak of this three-cornered relationship and the enormity of disruption to life created by Britain's heel on its two colonial jewels. But history will tell us that there was plenty of bad blood and spilled blood. For instance, during the 1964 Revolution on the island, intended as an intervention into the domination of the Arab/Asian ruling class, an estimated 5,000–12,000 Zanzibaris of Arab descent and several thousand ethnic Arab and Indian civilians were killed. Many more thousands were detained or expelled and their homes, businesses and coveted vehicles were confiscated or destroyed. Jetha Lila – a private bank operated by the descendants of Jetha Liladhar, a Bombay Bhatia merchant who opened it as a firm to operate as commission agents in 1880 – was forced to close by 1968, though the Revolution's leaders wished for it to remain open, because most of its Indian clientele had fled, fearing for their safety.

Conveying Vulnerability, the Possibility of Decay

Bhimji also includes photographs of several vehicles, which are she says, 'metaphors for revolution'. Notably, there are photographs of a 1951 Austin Princess limousine – the official grand transport of the Resident Governor of Zanzibar – and a Ford Zephyr. The significance of the Austin Princess, in particular, and its function in conveying the power of appointed officials, adds to our understanding of the aura surrounding these objects, and why they became 'metaphors for revolution'. Launched n 1947, the Princess was the most expensive flagship model in the Austin range; the standard version came in at almost two tonnes, and was 16'9" long, 6'1" wide. Because they were more modern in style than similar-sized Bentleys or Rolls-Royces and because their price came in at little more than two-thirds of the Rolls-Royce, they were favoured as an official state vehicle by appointed officials. Both the Princess and the Zephyr were abandoned by the last Resident Governor, who left in a hurry during the 1964 Revolution – in which Sheik Abeid Karume deposed Sultan Jamshid bin Abdullah, following Zanzibar's Independence in 1963. In April 1972, Karume, now a burly 67-year-old leftist strongman, was himself deposed from rule – legend states that, at the time, he was sitting down to play cards and sip coffee with old-time supporters. He, too, no doubt, left behind a car – a lesser car that speaks of infinitely lesser dreams than that of a grand and over-reaching empire.

Bhimji remains preoccupied with vulnerability and decay; she specifies, 'I did not choose the materials for their sensual qualities. I am attracted more to their vulnerability, the possibility of decay'.[13] That interest is evident in the photographs of the cars left behind by various Zanzibari rulers. For instance, the dust-encrusted Austin Princess and Ford Zephyr, their interiors dense with grids of cobwebs, are meditations on impermanence. Even whilst they present us with the opportunity to contemplate decay and forgetting, these symbolically powerful objects continue to have an impact on our psychologies and influence how we place ourselves in the world; we remain enthralled with their symbolic power, the freedom and authority they communicate. We, in the ex-colonies and Britain alike, continue to be trained into believing that British engineering and manufacturing is an unparalleled and marvellous thing – all of which is essential to constructing the structures of the British brand of white supremacy. Contradictorily, perhaps, these luxurious objects also contain the promise of re-animation and rebirth, through an entirely new set of avatars. Bhimji's photographs reveal that these rusting vehicles have been transformed into places of security for entire communities of spiders, who, through creating networks of entrapment for hapless insects, make life possible for future generations of their own.

Amplifying the Echoes of History

Whilst writing this, I read obituaries in honour of the US historian Hayden White (1928–2018), and realised that Bhimji's art works in concert with this groundbreaking scholar's writing. White focussed, from the beginning of his career, on the ways in which the narrative choices that each narrator makes have dramatic impacts on how we understand history. He stressed that historical meaning is created through choices we make, to include particular historical facts or utilise particular narrative structures, both of which are dependent on the narrator-historian's ethical and political standing. He coined the term 'emplotment' to define the ways in which one's choice of narrative structure – where one chooses to begin, end or include in the middle – will impose significance and meaning. White also argued, in one of his earliest essays, that whilst historians were required in the past to construct 'a specious continuity between the present world and that which preceded it', we have come to a time in which we 'require a history that will educate us to discontinuity more than ever before; for discontinuity, disruption and chaos is our lot.'[14] Much later in his life as a scholar, he advocated for the ways in which memory – attached as it were to decaying structures and residue left behind by the past – shaped what we construct as history, rather than the history that official narratives maintain is 'real' and significant.

Bhimji's return to this location – to East Africa and Zanzibar in particular – and the photographic works in *Lead White* are attempts to make the archives speak, to amplify the echoes that history left behind. They are a visual rendition of Hayden White's directives for historians, mediating the distance between official history and the embodied histories that our collective memories and bodies remember. By presenting us with a fragmented, elusive narrative structure, her work encourages us to question the grand and seamless narrative of history as we have learned it. Her focalisation on minutiae and imprinted matter in particular, reconfigures how history is read and how we read ourselves within this history.

Often, it is only leaking ink – peeking through on the underside of a piece of paper – that suggests the existence of those othered narratives; here, tied up with strings, imprinted by the impression left by seals bearing the state's coat of arms, lie the histories of the silenced and suppressed. When we see an image of a document bearing the seal of the Government of India, and 'Secret No. 15' handwritten in black India ink, we know that there were 14 secrets before it, and surely, many that followed. The word 'BULLETS', in capital letters, handwritten using black ink, feathers out into a deceptive softness on cheap, foolscap paper. This single word forces us out of the abstractions of history. It indicates that history stamped itself into someone's body: ordered and paid for, recorded neatly on poor-quality paper by some bureaucrat's hand and ending someone's life.

1
Bhimji, Zarina, email to M. Neelika Jayawardane,
29 March 2018.

2
Ibid.

3
Ibid.

4
Ibid.

5
From a WhatsApp conversation between M. Neelika
Jayawardane and Zarina Bhimji, January 2018.

6
Bhimji, Zarina, email to M. Neelika Jayawardane,
11 May 2018.

7
Bhimji, Zarina, email to M. Neelika Jayawardane,
8 March 2018.

8
Bhimji, Zarina, email to M. Neelika Jayawardane,
29 March 2018.

9
Ibid.

10
Bhimji, Zarina, email to M. Neelika Jayawardane,
8 March 2018.

11
Bhimji, Zarina, email to M. Neelika Jayawardane,
29 March 2018.

12
Battiscombe, Edward, *Trees and Shrubs of Kenya
Colony*, Nairobi: Government Printers, 1936.

13
Boyce, Sonia, 'Conversation with Zarina Bhimji' in *Zarina
Bhimji: I will always be here*, (Birmingham: Ikon Gallery,
1991).

14
White, Hayden V, "The Burden of History" in *History and
Theory*, Vol. 5, No. 2 (1966), pp. 111–134 http://abuss.
narod.ru/Biblio/white_burden.htm.

BRITISH PROTEST

The postcards whispered, very quietly, a question: 'Do you know why the bombardment in 1896 happened?' A long silence followed, then another question came: 'Why was Arab power weakened?' Fatima replied, 'Why do you ask me these questions? Yesterday the camera asked me why the British abolished slavery.' The postcards seemed anxious to reply yet they did not. Fatima quietly and swiftly began to read the words in front of her:

> Dominion office, German Emperor, Mackinnon, Slavery and slave trade, land decree, Bombay correspondence, Political and Secret Dept, Postal rules, Government of India Correspondence, Register of freed slaves, treaty between queen and sultan, crown of Italy, crown agents, The English club, Baron von der Decken, Topan, German treaty, 1839 Treaty, British witness, Deed of freedom of slave, Uganda company, Uganda protectorate, Arabic correspondence, Residency, Foreign affairs, British Imperial East Africa, Uganda Protectorate, land office, the land acquisition act 1909, land alienation decree, land protection decree. claims to land, German consular records, German Empire, Legislation decrees, Sultan records from the palace, Arabic script, Maritime Bureau, probate records, Merikani, Kaniki from India, Barsati from India, cloves, informal empire, Angola Zanzibar war, Gerhard Rohlfs 1885, German Consul General, German East Africa Company (Deutsch-Ostafrikanische Gesellschaft), German Consulate, Baron Von Rechenberg, indirect rule, Her Majesty, British occupation, Swaziland, Harry Holdsworth Rawson (1843–1910), Bombardment, Frank Beardmore and company, Foreign dictation, Alien colonial rule, friendly relations with China, Independence, The Berlin conference, Congo conference, Bhuj court, Government House, Nyasaland, Southern Rhodesia, Book of free slaves, Relative to slave dhows, confidential, European staff, international agreement, Secret, secret department, Calcutta, Crown London, Plantation, Madam, Mrs Marshall-May, humble servant, India office, Portuguese colonies…

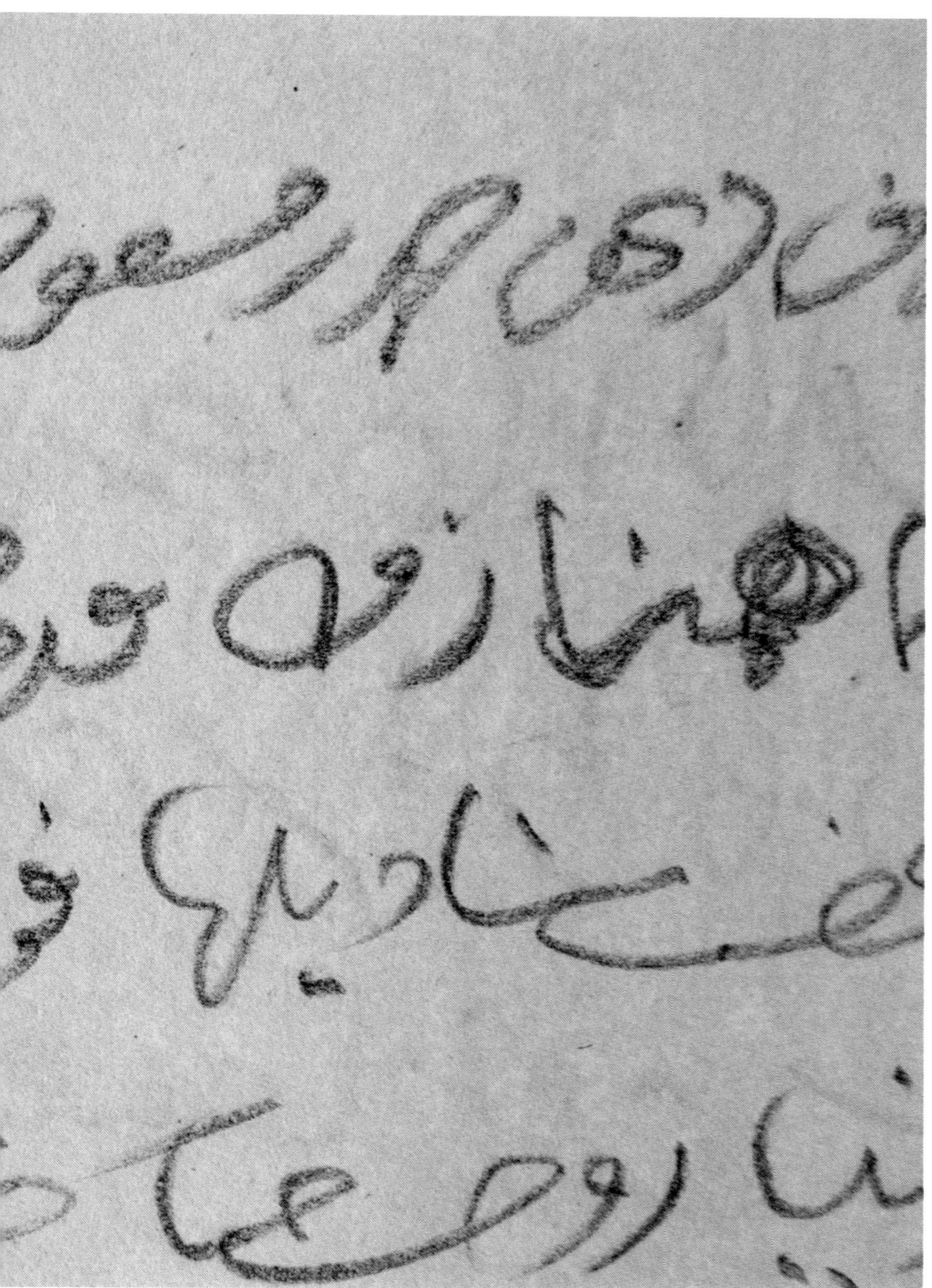

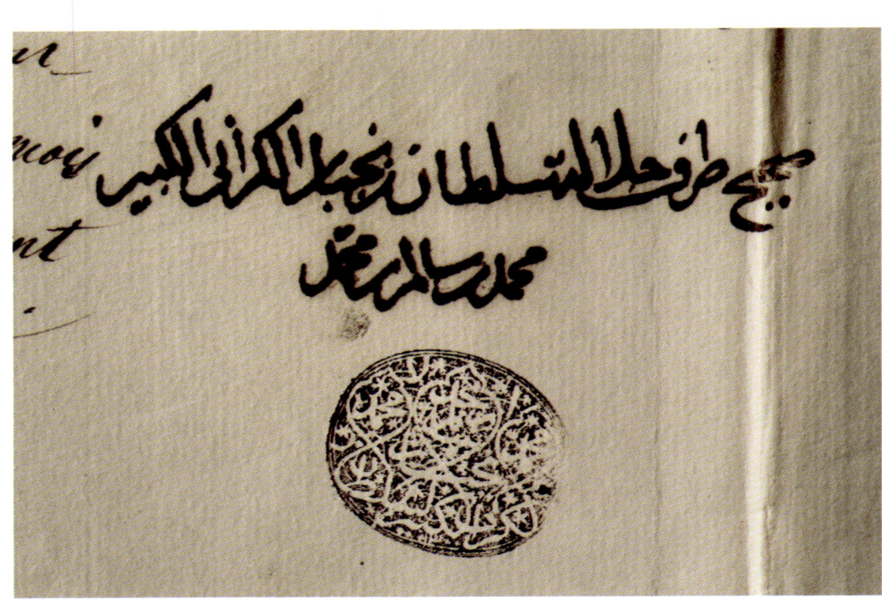

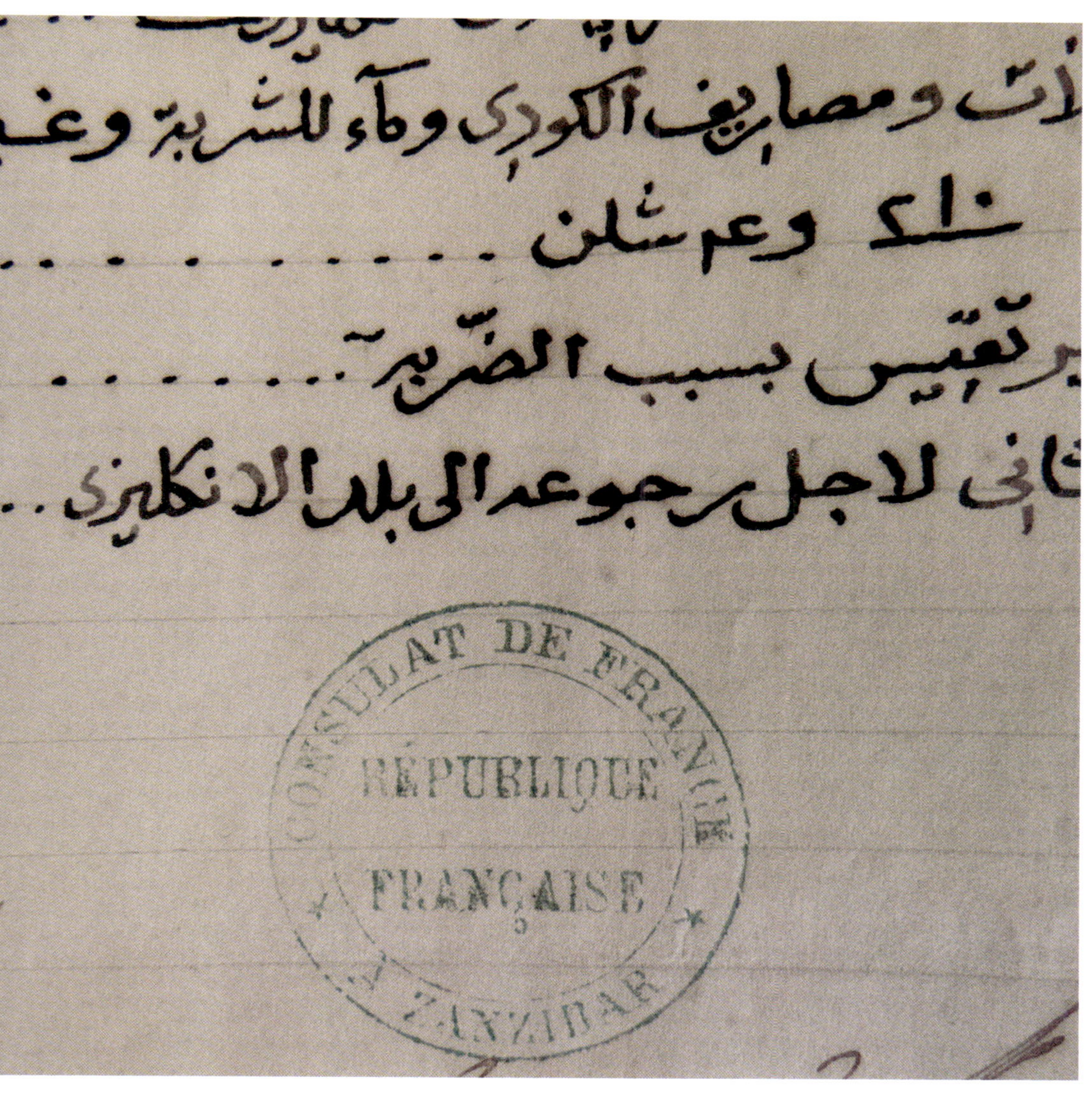

ت ومصاريف الكوري وماء للشربة وغ

ذلك وعم شلن . . . .

تعيين بسبب الضريبة . . . .

انى لاجل رجوعه الى بلد الانكليزى . . .

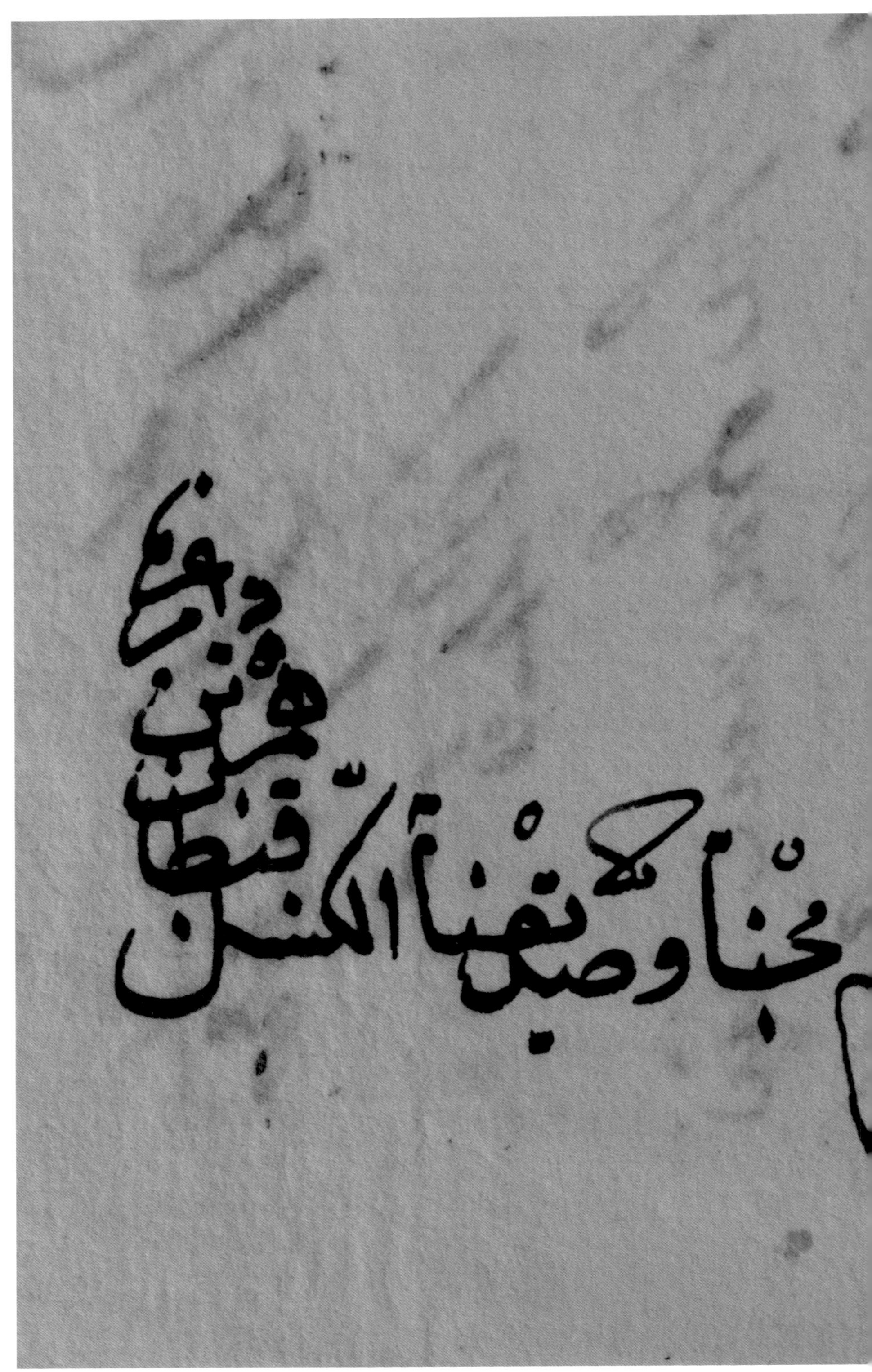

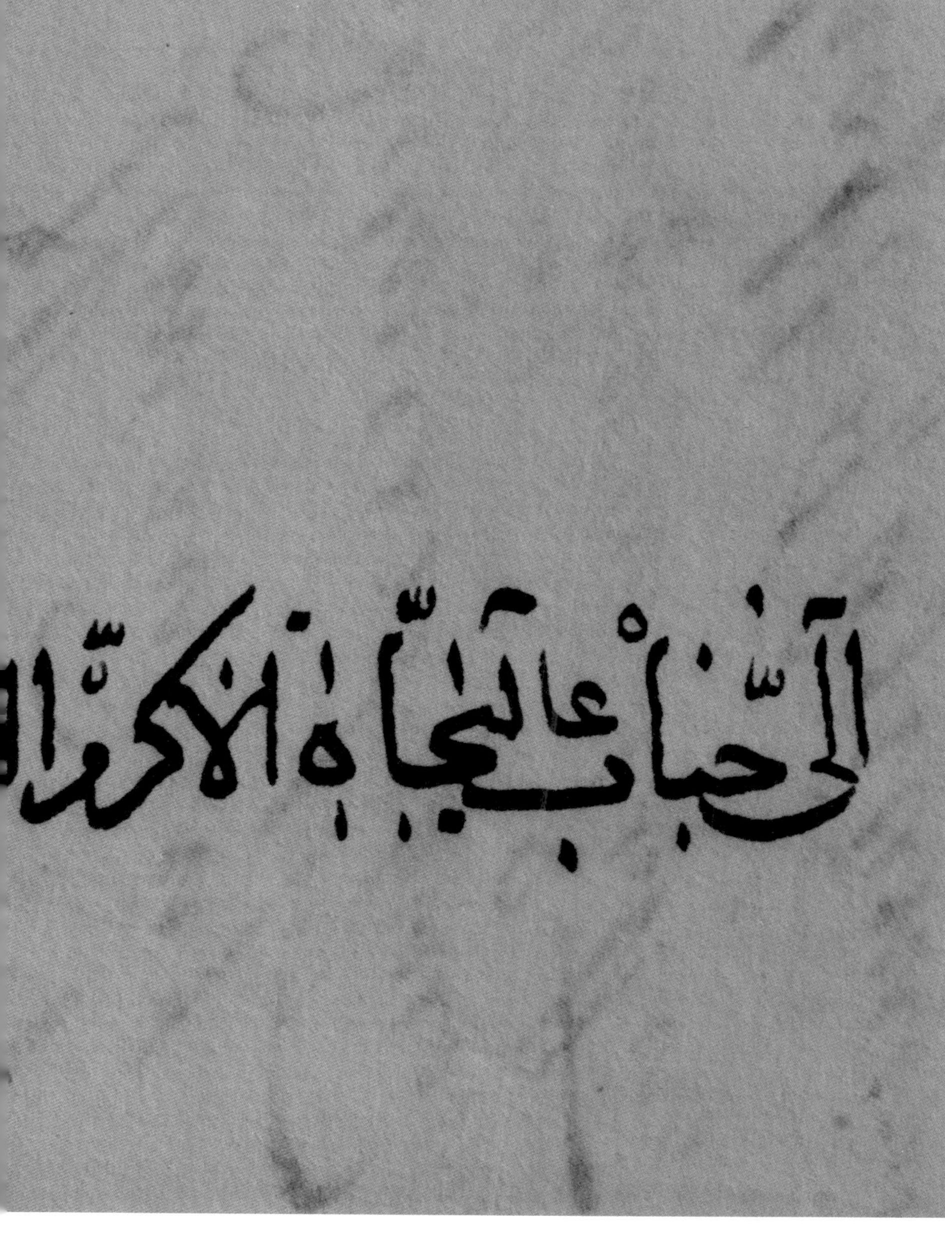

10s BROWN

The stamp asked the question: 'Are you looking at the crime?' The camera replied, 'It is not important who the murderer is or who the victim is.' It was not until the next day that the camera added: 'It is not important to think how he killed or carried out his crime. The crime is only the beginning.' As the days went by the camera continued thinking: 'The important question is why society produced such a crime. The crime enabled him to be a hero and this transformed him. How is it that a peaceful person can be transformed into a monster?' The camera wondered how someone could be capable of committing something truly dreadful. But should the question really be about society and not about the crime?

There is tension growing within the archives, and some of the documents – especially many that have been overlooked – are growing agitated.

The police were working for the State and not for the people.

The murderer is trying to find a way out. There is moral ambiguity; he is a greedy, selfish person under political and economic pressure. Being honest to himself is really difficult in these circumstances.

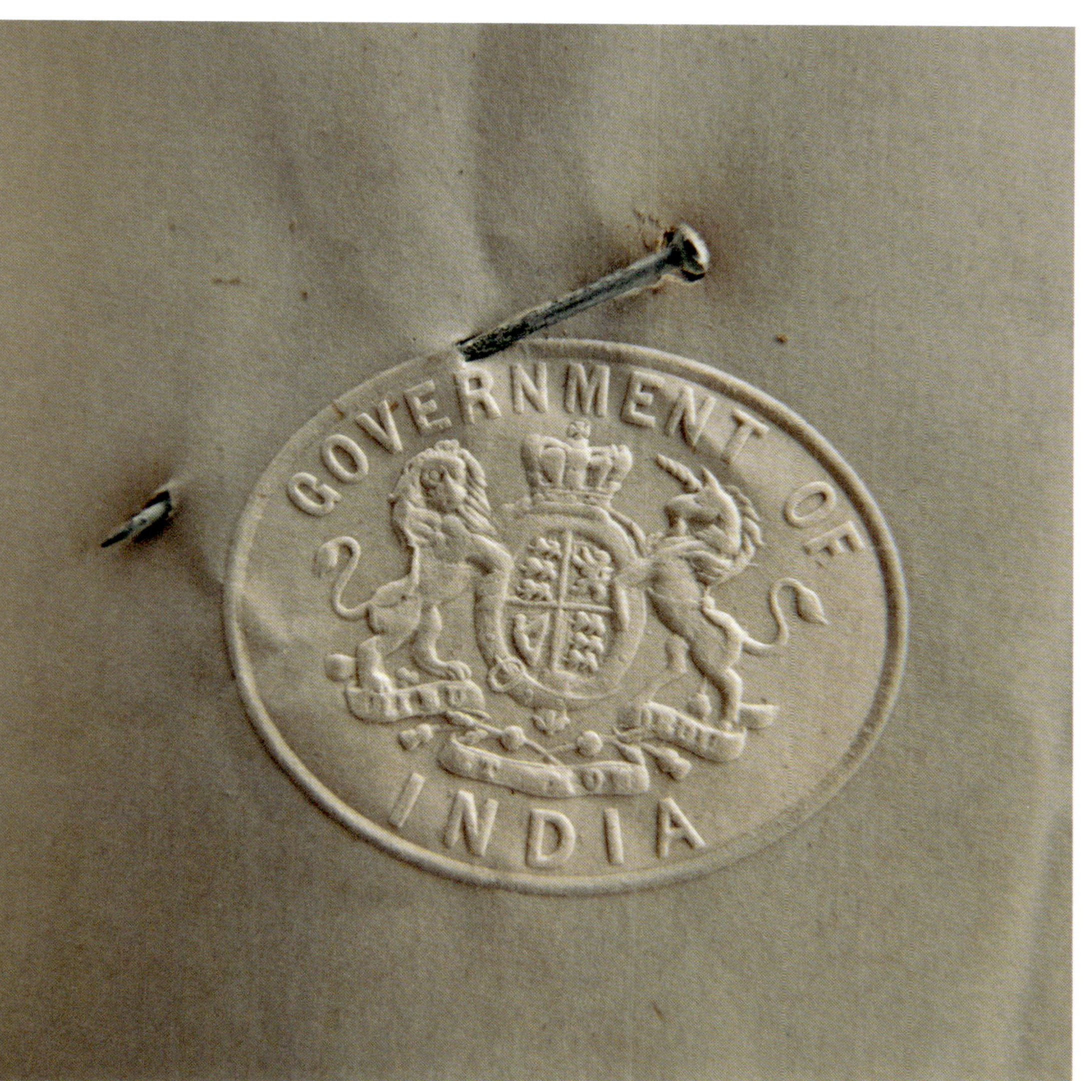
GOVERNMENT OF
INDIA

FOREIGN DEPT
GOVT OF INDIA

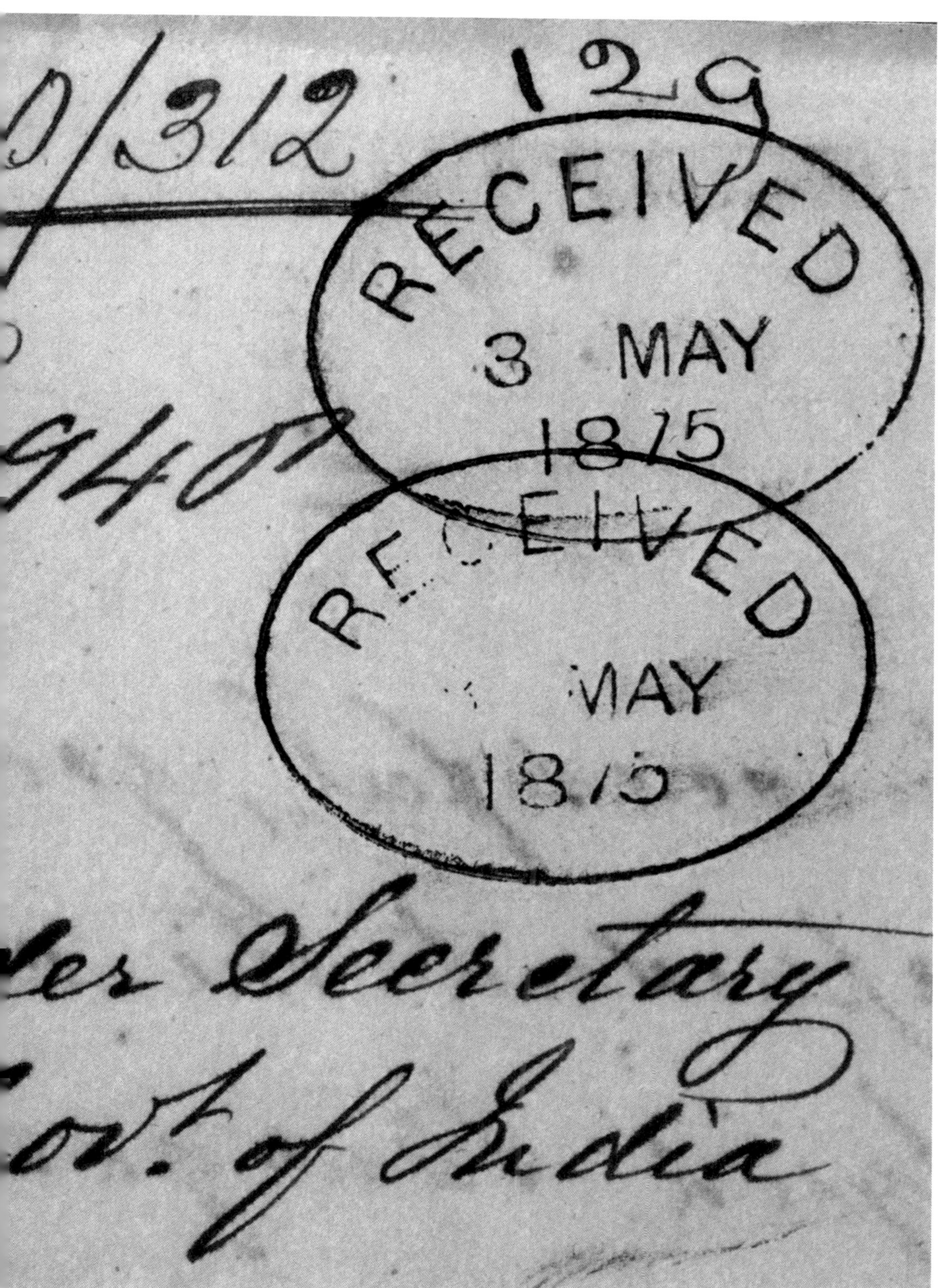
RECEIVED
3 MAY
1815
RECEIVED
MAY
1815

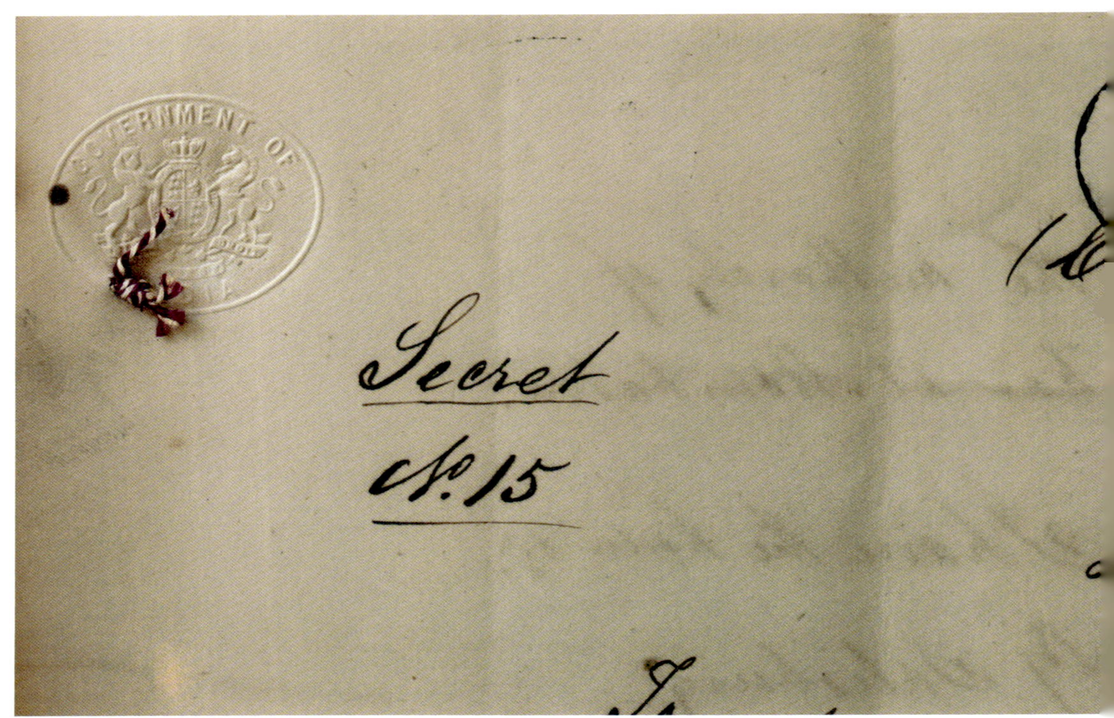
Secret
Nº 15

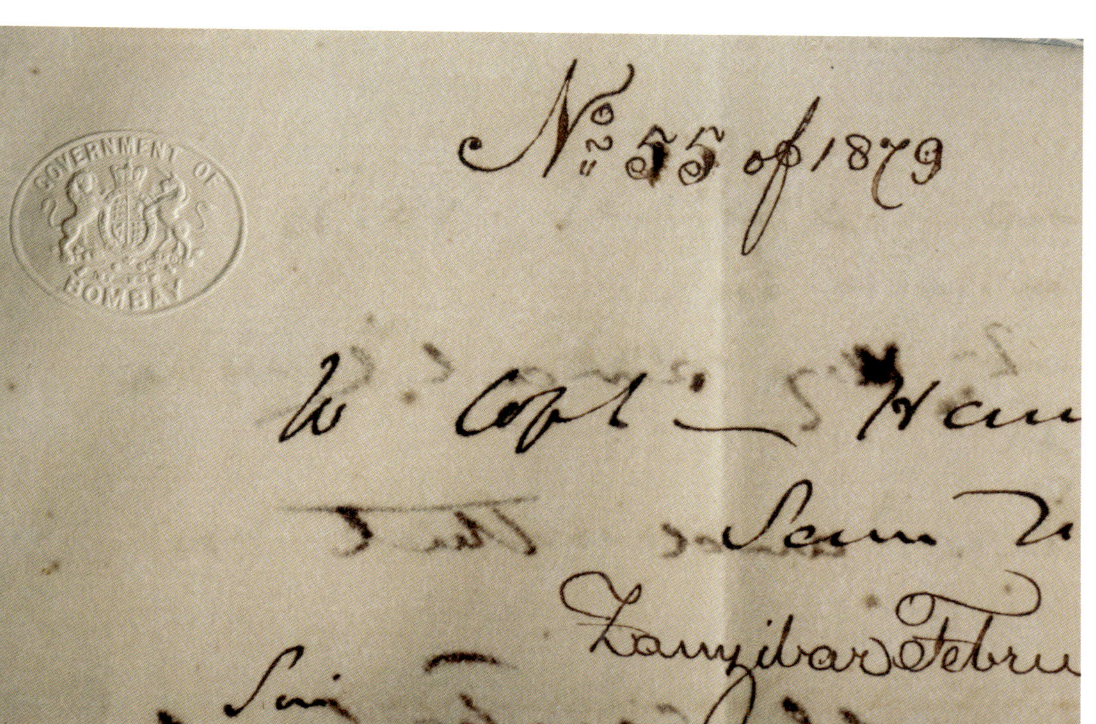

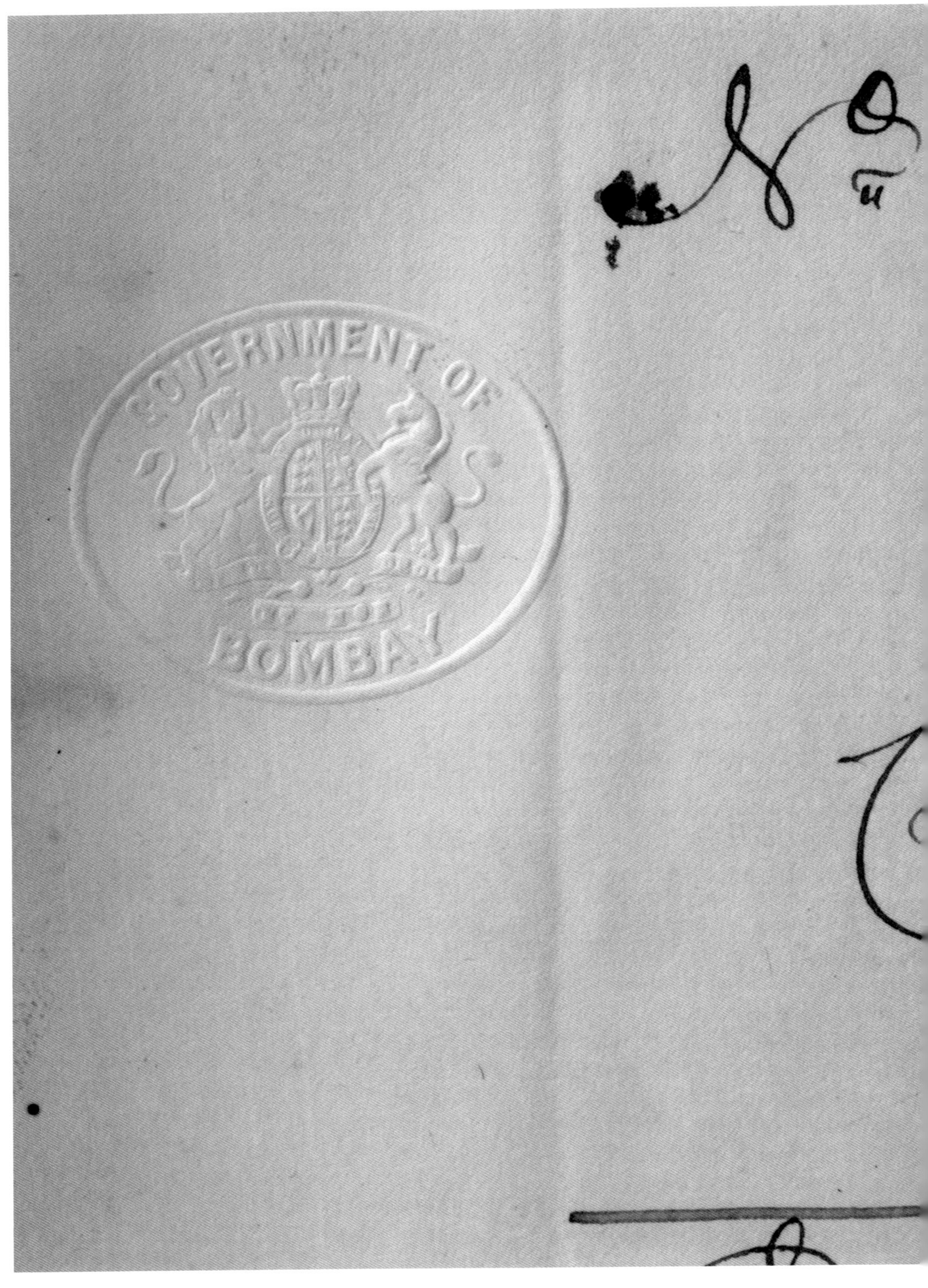

$\dfrac{82}{78}$ of 1875.

U aitch

NEEDLEWORK

After the bombardment things got very busy. Officers put the needles to work, marking out the words.

BRITISH WEST AFRICA
(Sierra Leone, Colony and protectorate)

BRITISH WEST AFRICA
(Gold Coast colony, with Ashanti and protectorate, northern territories)

SOUTHERN NIGERIA PROTECTORATE AND NORTHERN NIGERIA

BRITISH SOUTH AND CENTRAL AFRICA

BRITISH SOUTH AFRICA
(Cape of Good Hope)

BRITISH SOUTH AFRICA
(Natal, including Zululand and Amatongaland)

BRITISH SOUTH AFRICA
(Bechuanaland protectorate)
(see also Rhodesia)

BRITISH SOUTH AFRICA
(Orange River Colony, formerly Orange Free State)

BRITISH SOUTH AFRICA
(Transvaal)

BRITISH SOUTH AFRICA
(Swaziland)

BRITISH SOUTH AFRICA
RHODESIA, Viz:-
  (1) SOUTHERN RHODESIA
  (2) NORTHERN RHODESIA
  (3) Barotziland-North-Western Rhodesia
  (4) North-Eastern Rhodesia

BRITISH CENTRAL AFRICA
(Nyasaland and protectorate)

BRITISH EAST AFRICA
(Zanzibar Protectorate)
(East Africa Protectorate)
(Uganda Protectorate)
(Somaliland Protectorate)

BRITISH EAST AFRICA
(Uganda Protectorate)

BRITISH EAST AFRICA
(Somaliland Protectorate)

SOCOTRA
(British Protection)

ABYSSINIA &c.

Africa (central) to Comoro Islands

CONGO, BELGIAN
SOUTHERN NIGERIA PROTECTORATE AND NORTHERN NIGERIA
DENMARK AND GREAT BRITAIN
DENMARK AND CONGO
EGYPT (AND SOUDAN)
FRANCE AND ABYSSINIA
FRANCE (EAST AFRICA)
FRANCE (WEST AFRICA)
FRANCE (ALGERIA)
GERMANY, GREAT BRITAIN AND FRANCE
GREAT BRITAIN AND GERMANY
GREAT BRITAIN AND ITALY
GREAT BRITAIN, GERMANY AND ITALY
GREAT BRITAIN AND LIBERIA
GREAT BRITAIN AND MOROCCO
GREAT BRITAIN AND NETHERLANDS
GREAT BRITAIN AND PORTUGAL
GREAT BRITAIN AND TURKEY, UNITED STATES

Surveillance of international, No power shall exercise rights of sovereignty, hostilities not to be extended to neutralized states, British engagements, rules of navigation to be established, Great Britain not restricted from making any rules not contrary to above engagements, signatory powers, fire arms and ammunition, protection to natives, protection of mission, British Protectorate, foreign powers, Future occupations, African Slave trade by land and sea, General Act, Brussels Act, A declaration, Adhering powers, Declarations &c., Foreign Powers, full power, Properties rights, Native power, 'Berlin Act', Possessions in Africa, Great Powers, Our ancestors, authority, dispose, Abandon, relinquish, dominions, Non purchase or sale of slaves, Domestic servitude, Treaties with Native, British and German spheres, limits, Territorial arrangement, delimited, native claims, 'British Subject' Acts of cession by native chiefs, Powers for purpose, lands, foreign powers, slavery, Question of Title, Native Land Owners,

Foregoing Privilege, Cession to Great Britain, Dutch East India, European colonists, Privileges of every white male in Swaziland, every white person admitted to the privileges, Rights of Crown, Musulman Power, Authority Over Musulmans, Mahommedan Law, power of company to acquire and possess lands &c, Suppression of the slave trade and slavery, Slave raiding, Declaration Relative to the Slave Trade, Prevention of Sale or Shipment of Slave, Slave Coast, Liberated Slaves, Supervision Over Native Vessels, Embarkation of Negro Passengers, Negro Passengers, Landing of Negro Passengers, Slaves on board for sale exportation or importation, people for sale, or exchange as slaves, Importation of coolie Labour, claims to Lands, Houses, or Sambas, Runaway slaves, Umpire, Sanction of the crown, It was my intention to be silent, been misplaced, misapprehension, Engagements of British Subjects of Natives of Madagascar, Leases, Contracts &c., Duty on Cotton Goods, Demarcation of Spheres of influence, English Trading Privileges, Treatment of Native Chiefs, England will not obstruct France in Morocco, French Rights in Egypt to be respected, Lines of Demarcation, Protection of Missionaries, fresh Determination, Astronomical Determination, Moon – Culminating stars, Occultation, High-Water Mark, 'Deep Water Line', Statements of Natives, Median line, Claim, Ownership, Portuguese Occupation, Preserve, intact, Rights of the British Crown, Queen of England, Queen of Great Britain and Ireland, Her Most Gracious Majesty Victoria (of Great Britain & Ireland), Empress of India, God Save the Queen, Victoria by the Grace of God, Her Majesty the Queen-Empress, Government of His Britannic Majesty…

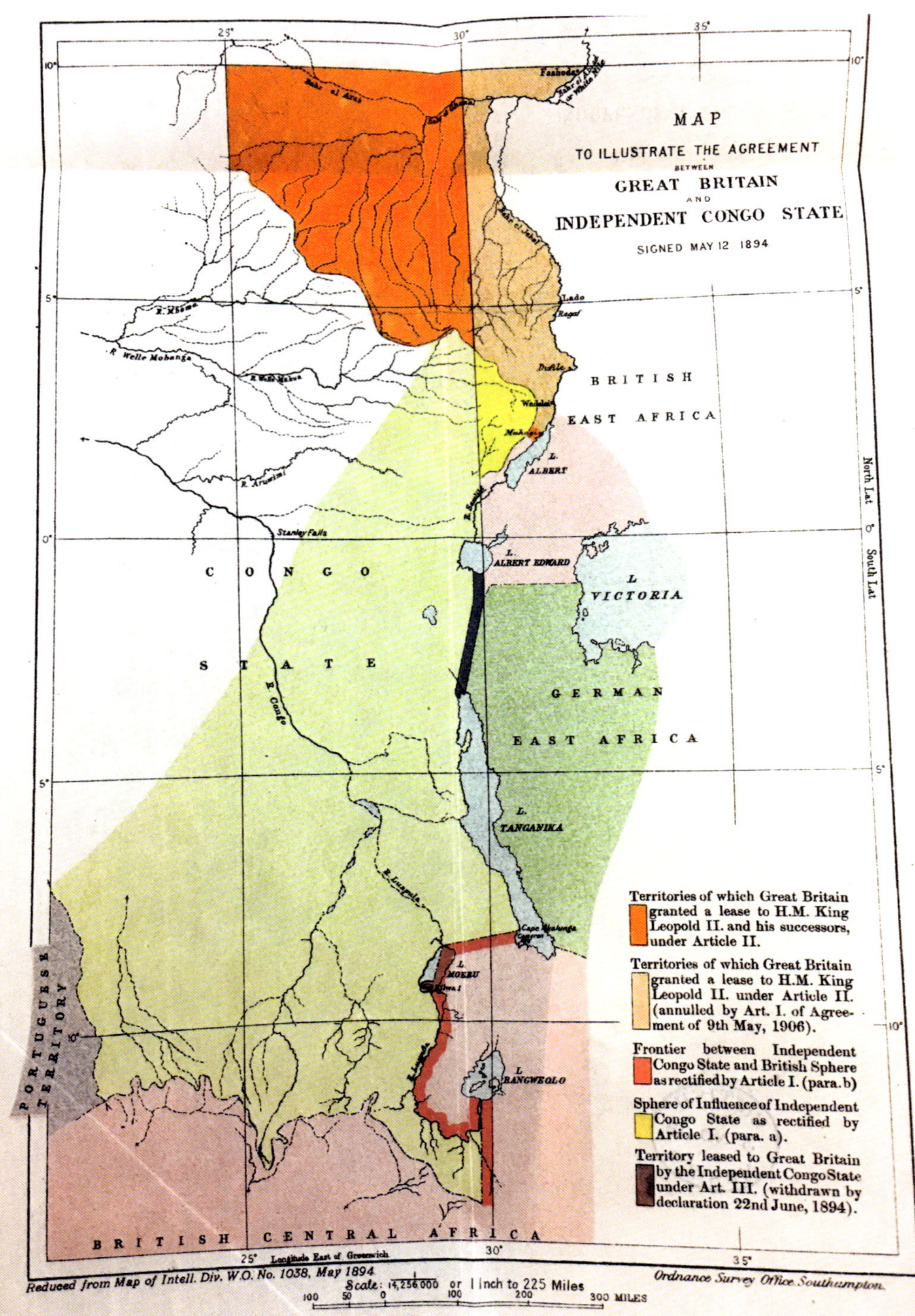
MAP
TO ILLUSTRATE THE AGREEMENT
BETWEEN
GREAT BRITAIN
AND
INDEPENDENT CONGO STATE
SIGNED MAY 12 1894

Fashoda
Lado
Regaf
Dufile
Wadelai
Mahagi
L. ALBERT
BRITISH
EAST AFRICA
L. ALBERT EDWARD
L. VICTORIA
GERMAN
EAST AFRICA
L. TANGANIKA
Cape Makunga
L. MOERU
L. BANGWEOLO
PORTUGUESE TERRITORY
CONGO STATE
Stanley Falls
R. Aruwimi
R. Welle Makua
R. Welle Mobanga
R. Mbomu
Bahr el Arab
R. Lualaba
R. Congo
BRITISH CENTRAL AFRICA

North Lat.
South Lat.

Territories of which Great Britain
granted a lease to H.M. King
Leopold II. and his successors,
under Article II.

Territories of which Great Britain
granted a lease to H.M. King
Leopold II. under Article II.
(annulled by Art. I. of Agreement of 9th May, 1906).

Frontier between Independent
Congo State and British Sphere
as rectified by Article I. (para. b)

Sphere of Influence of Independent
Congo State as rectified by
Article I. (para. a).

Territory leased to Great Britain
by the Independent Congo State
under Art. III. (withdrawn by
declaration 22nd June, 1894).

Reduced from Map of Intell. Div. W.O. No. 1038, May 1894
Scale: 1:14,256,000 or 1 Inch to 225 Miles
100 50 0 100 200 300 MILES
Longitude East of Greenwich
Ordnance Survey Office Southampton.

Railways
in construction
Telegraphs
British
French
German
Portuguese
Liberia
Spanish
1
6,336,000 or 1 Inch to 100
100

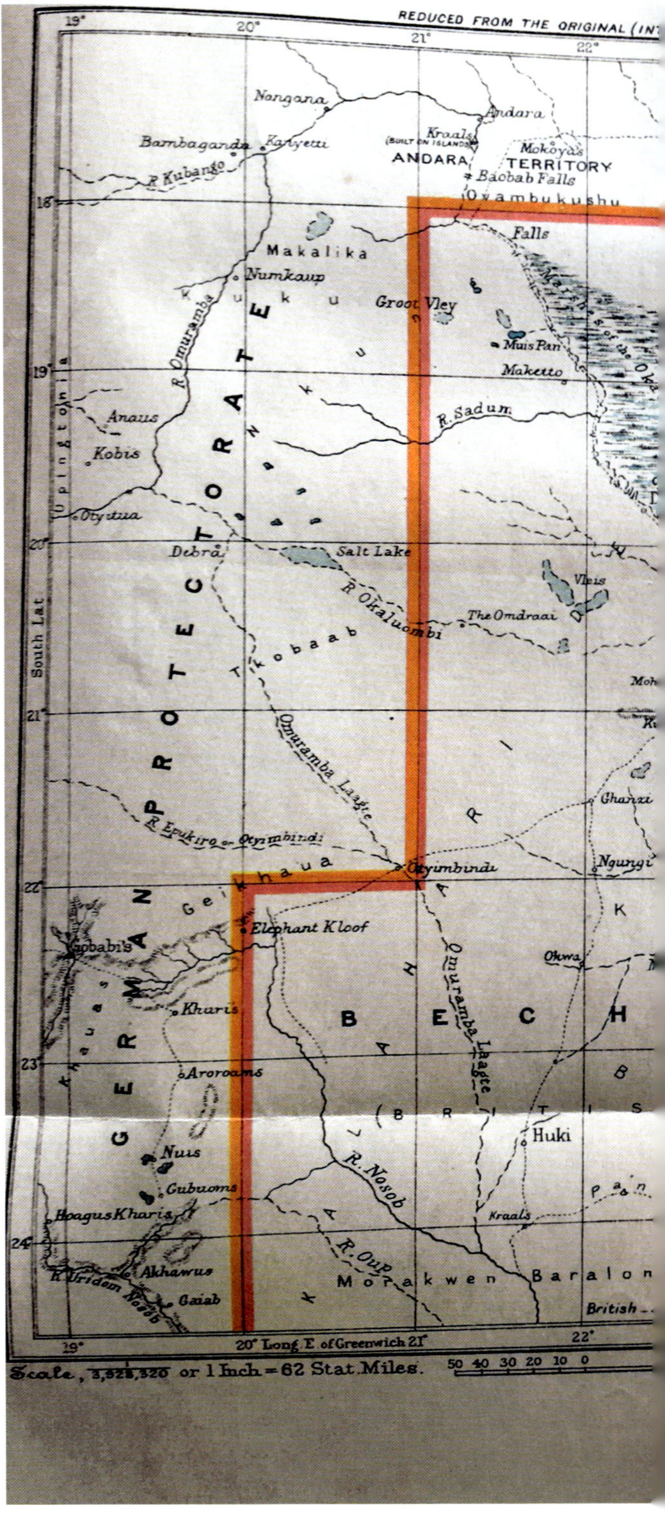
REDUCED FROM THE ORIGINAL (INT
19°
20°
21°
22°
Nangana
Andara
Bambaganda
Kanyetti
Kraals
(BUILT ON ISLANDS)
Mokoya's
R. Kubango
ANDARA
TERRITORY
Baobab Falls
18°
Oxambukushu
Makalika
Falls
Numkaup
K u k u
Groot Vley
Muis Pan
R. Omuramba
u
Maketto
19°
u
Anaus
k
R. Sadum
Upington
Kobis
N
South Lat.
Otyiua
20°
Debra
Salt Lake
Vleis
R. Okaluombi
The Omdraai
Moh
21°
Kobaab
K
Ki
P
R
O
T
E
C
T
O
R
A
T
E
I
Omuramba Laagte
R
Ghanzi
R. Epukiro
Otyimbindi
Ngungi
Geikhaua
Otyimbindi
22°
G
E
R
M
A
N
Elephant Kloof
K
Gobabis
Omuramba Laagte
Okwa
M
Khauas
Kharis
B
E
C
H
H
23°
Aroroams
A
B
Huki
Nuis
R. Nosob
Pan
Gubuoms
Kraals
Hoagus Kharis
A
British
24°
R. Uriden
Akhawus
Morakwen
Baralon
Nosob
Gaiab
K
R. Oup
British
19°
20° Long. E. of Greenwich 21°
22°
Scale, 3,928,320 or 1 Inch = 62 Stat. Miles.
50 40 30 20 10 0

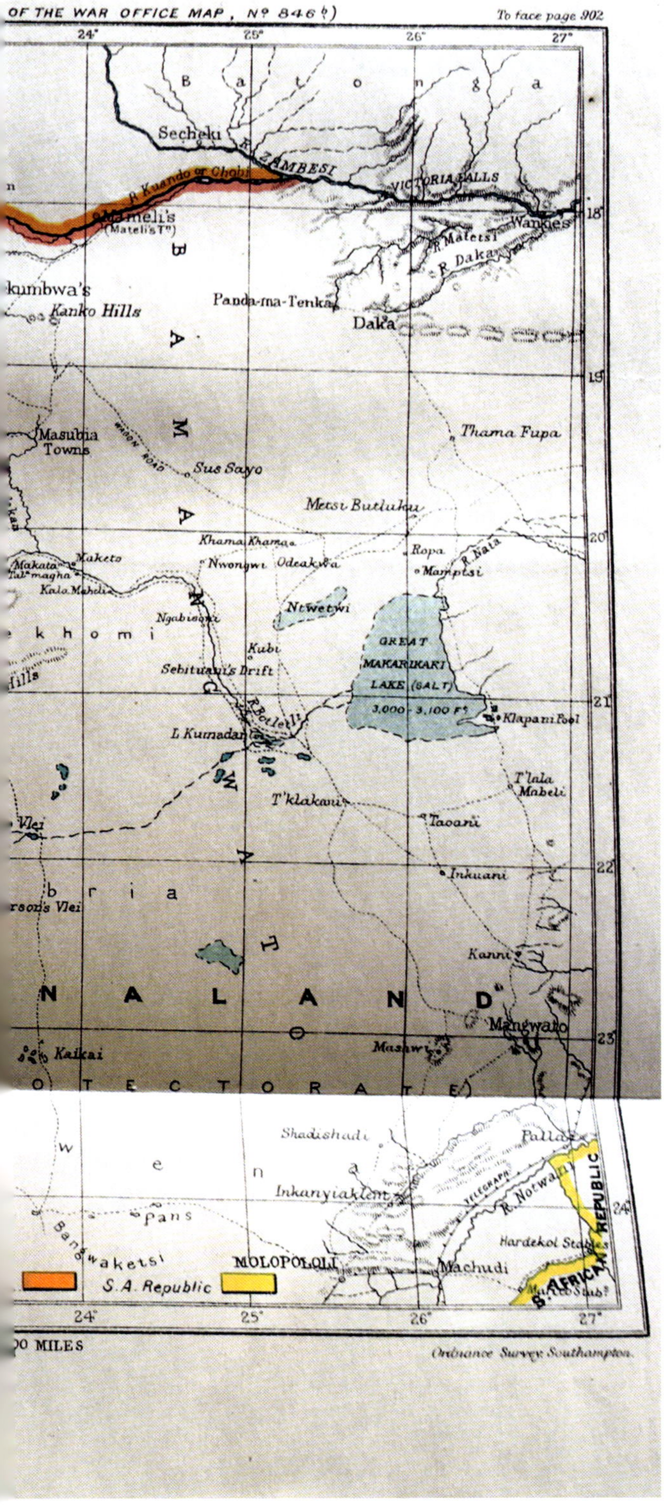
OF THE WAR OFFICE MAP , No 846b)
To face page 902
24°
25°
26°
27°
B   A   T   O   N   g   a
Secheku
R. ZAMBESI
R. Kuando or Chobi
VICTORIA FALLS
Mameli's
(Mateli'sTn)
Wankie's
18°
R. Maletsi
R. Dakay
kumbwa's
Kanko Hills
Panda-ma-Tenka
Daka
B   A   M   A   N
19°
Masubia
Towns
Thama Fupa
Sus Sayo
Metsi Butluku
20°
Khama Khama
Ropa
R. Nata
Makets
Nwongwi   Odeakwa
Mamptsi
Makata
Tal-magha
Kala Mahdi
Ntwetwi
khomi
Ngabisowi
Kubi
GREAT
MAKARIKARI
LAKE (SALT)
3,000 - 3,100 F?
Hills
Sebituani's Drift
R. Botletli
21°
L. Kumadau
Klapani Pool
Vlei
T'klakani
T'lala
Mabeli
Taoani
bria
22°
sons Vlei
Inkuani
T
Kanni
N   A   L   A   N   D
Mangwato
23°
Kaikai
Masawi
O   T   E   C   T   O   R   A   T   E
Shadishadi
Palla
w
e
n
a
Inkanyiaklen
TELEGRAPH
R. Notwai
24°
Pans
Bamawakets'
MOLOPOLOLI
Machudi
Hardekol Stad
S. AFRICAN REPUBLIC
S.A. Republic
24°
25°
26°
27°
MILES
Ordnance Survey, Southampton

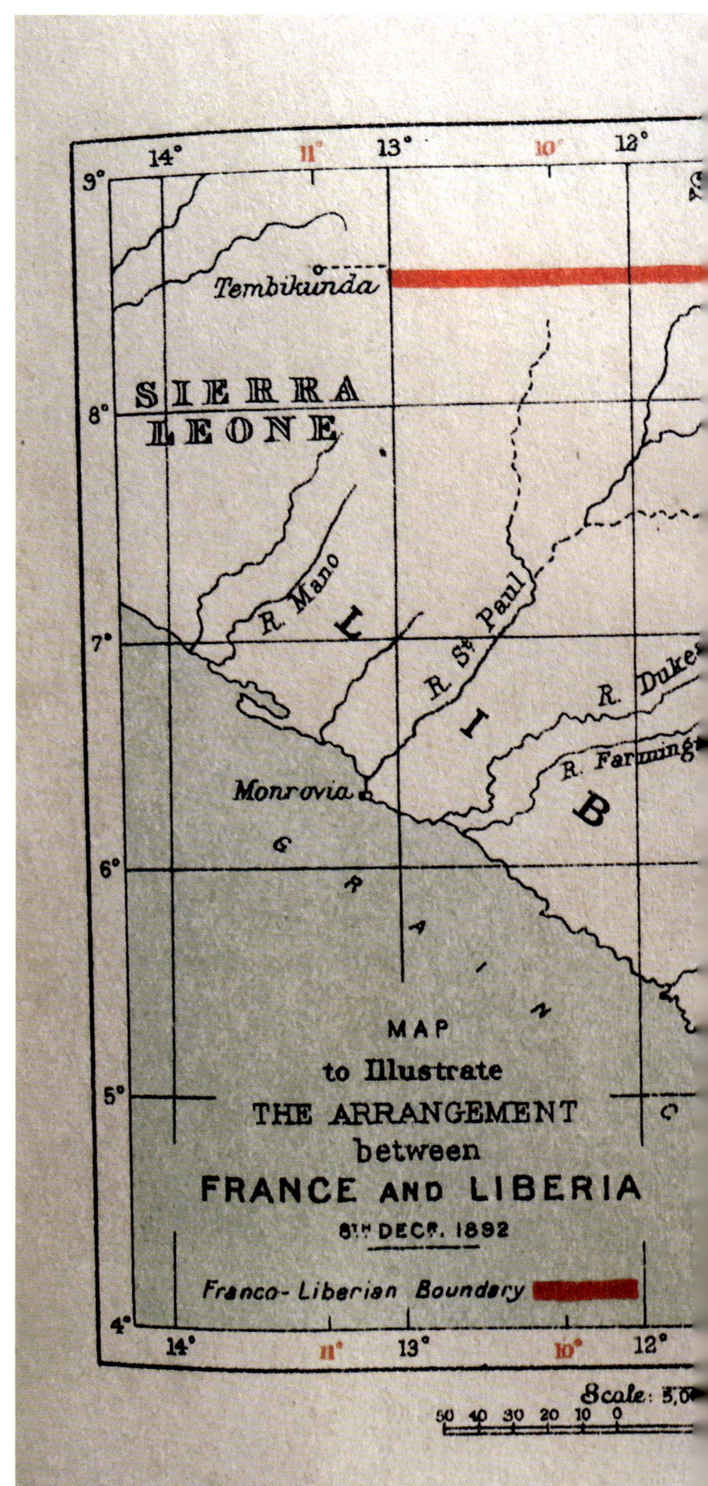
14°
11°
13°
10°
12°
9°
Tembikunda
SIERRA
LEONE
8°
R. Mano
R. St Paul
R. Duke
R. Farming
7°
L
I
Monrovia
B
G
6°
R
A
I
N
MAP
to Illustrate
THE ARRANGEMENT
between
FRANCE AND LIBERIA
6TH DECR. 1892
5°
C
Franco- Liberian Boundary
14°
11°
13°
10°
12°
4°
Scale: 5,0
50 40 30 20 10 0

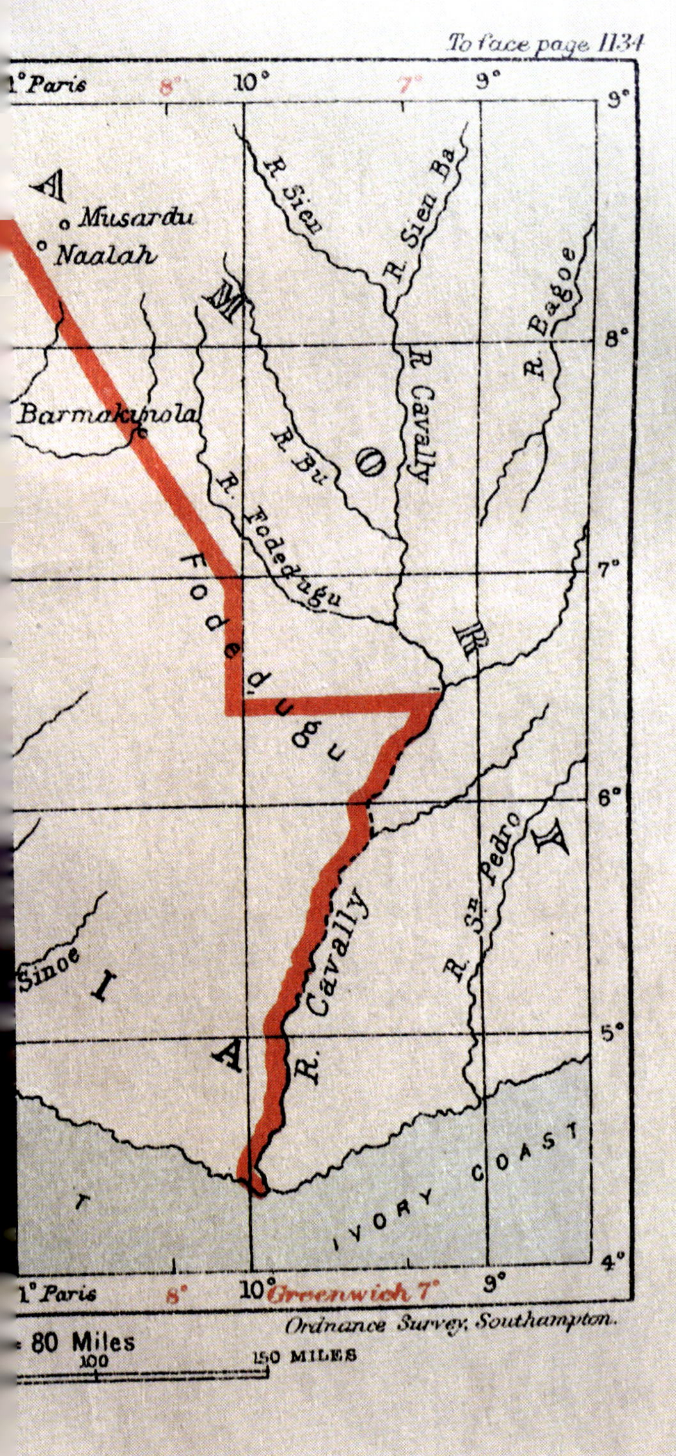
To face page 1134
1°Paris
8°
10°
7°
9°
9°
Musardu
Naalah
R. Sien
R. Sien Ba
R. Eagoe
M
8°
Barmakunola
R. Bu
R. Cavally
R. Fodedugu
O
7°
Fodedugu
R
6°
R. Sn Pedro
A
R. Cavally
Sinoe
I
5°
A
T
IVORY COAST
4°
1°Paris
8°
10°
Greenwich 7°
9°
Ordnance Survey, Southampton.
80 Miles
100
150 MILES

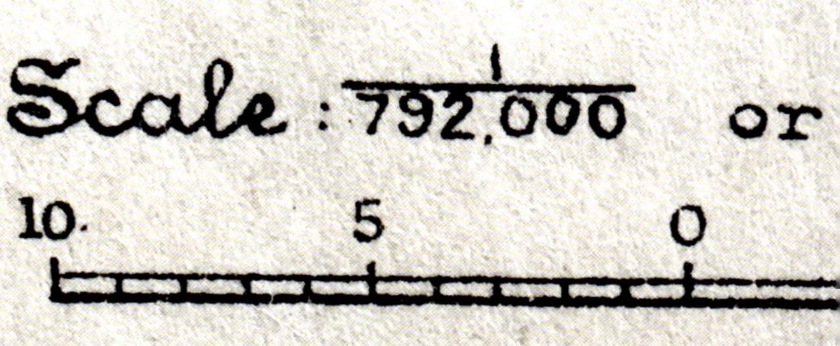
Scale : 1/792,000 or
10.   5   O
Britis
Frenc

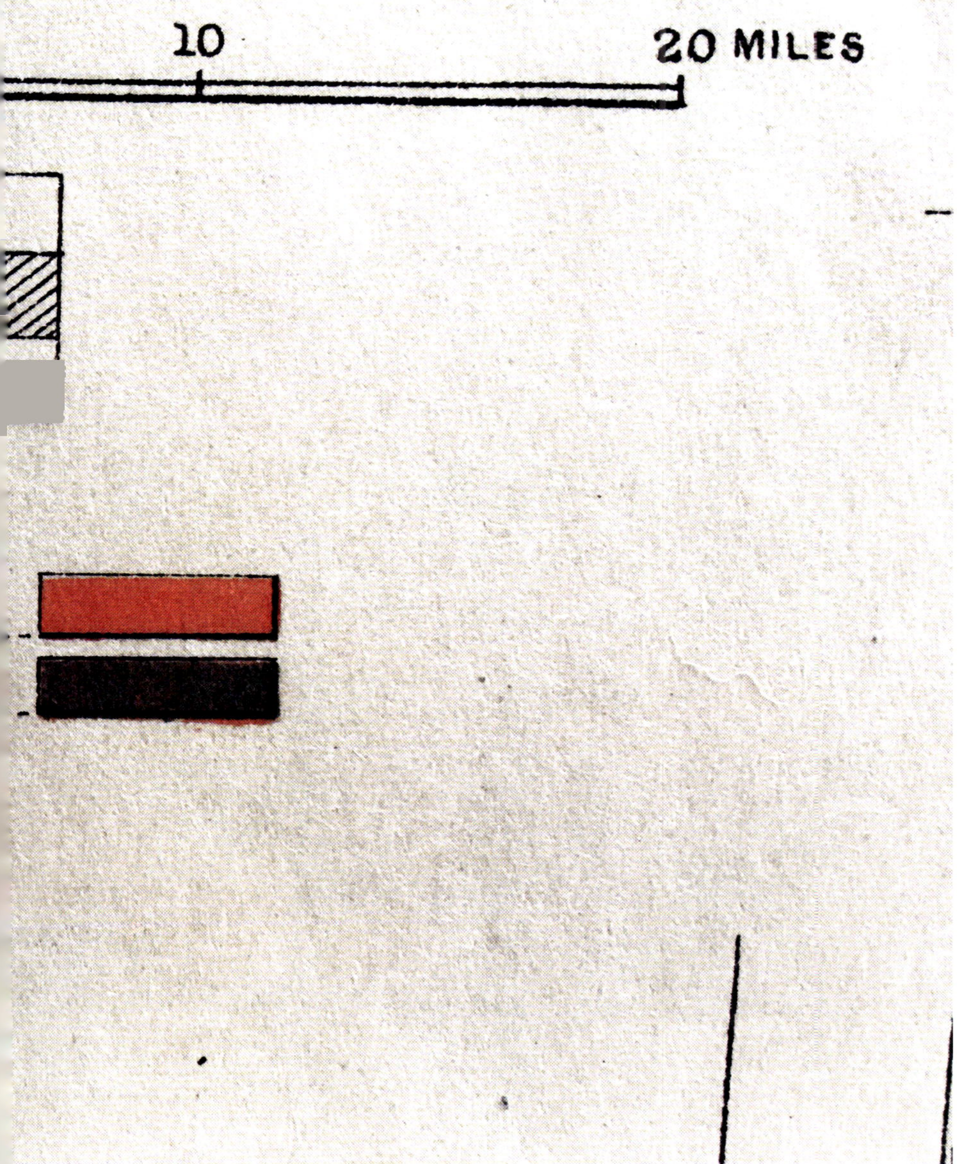
nch = 12·5 Stat. Miles
10
20 MILES

Misc. 27.

MOMBO.

12th April 1911.

Sir,

I have the honour to inform you that I have been
sentenced to 14 days imprisonment by the German court in
Tanga, in connection with my alleged "brutal" assault on a
rickshaw - boy in Tanga about last October.

The case was as follows:-

I hired a rickshaw ~~rxkxay~~ for 45 minutes and paid the boy
one rupee. on arrival at the Grand Hotel, Taanga, the boy
followed me onto the verandah and demanded another rupee,
I told him to go away but he refused . After a while I
called one of the Hotel boys, named Frederick, to remove
him but he absolutely declined to go and was decidedly impe-
rtinent in his manner. Whereupon I stood up and would have
boxed his ears but I saw two Germans on the verandah so I
refrained and pushed him with my foot instead, unfortunately
he was winded and was doubled up for a few seconds. At no
time did he fall to the ground. I left the hotel about twenty
minutes later whereupon, I am informed, the two Germans who ~~xxe~~
were on the verandah saw fit to interfere and called an ~~aikat~~
asikari to take the boy to hospital, in an ambulance. ~~Wil~~ whilst
on his way to the hospital, I have it on good authority, that
the rickshaw - boy ran away and was not seen for two days, ~~txx~~

2.

days, thus proving his injuries to be nil.

That night I heard about the Germans taking the boy to hospital so on the following morning I immediately went to the Court House to state the facts of the case as they really stood and my evidence was taken down, in full, in Kiswahili,

Some time afterwards I had the option of appearing in Court or otherwise but on the suggestion of our District Commissioner here I did not appear as he gave me to understand that it was unneccessary and that the case was about to be quashed.

In my opinion the whole case was nothing more than an expression of " Anti-British feeling, more especially as one of the men who reported me is a well known Anti-Britisher and his statement on his card which he presented to the Court to the effect that he had just witnessed a most brutal assault by an Englander on a Native was a most scurrilous inexactitude.

Mr Siegel, our District Commissioner here, states that he is quite prepared and willing to give evidence as to my methods of dealing with Natives.

I have made my appeal through Mr Rechtswalt Klockner of Tanga,

Britannic Majesty's
Vice Consul.
Dar es Salaam

I have the honour to be,

Sir,

Your obedient Servant   A.J. Montgomerie

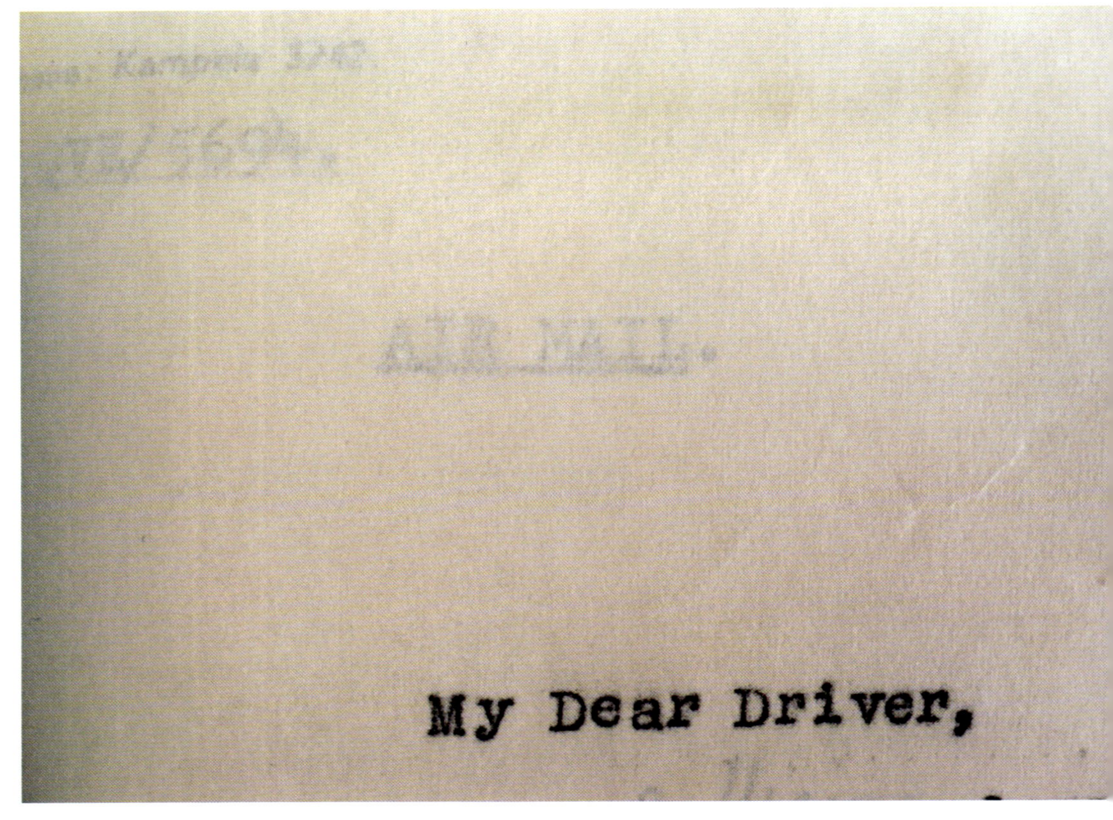
AIR MAIL.
My Dear Driver,

RESPECTING

THE BRITISH EAST

LICENSE TO FLY

Issued at the

Name of vessel ....*Zab*............

Name of Owner *Jarah Ada*....

Residence of Owner....*Zanzi*

Class of vessel ...... *Mtepe*....

RICA PROTECTORATE.

British
~~ZANZIBAR~~ FLAG.

Wassun...

.... {(Arabic)
                                       (English)}

a Madhani .... {(Arabic)
                                   (English)}

....

....

MINUTES.

As you no doubt know the present owner is
the son of Sir Tharia Topan and Lady Janbai and my
late partner Mr.Mead negotiated for the dedication
of what is now known as the Lady Janbai road (that
was a new road made through Lady Janbai's land) -
Lady Janbai has only recently given this property to
her son but I do not know how or when Sir Tharia
Topan acquired the land.

Failing the discovery of some further ----
authorities on Mahomedan Law the only possible ---
courses would appear to be either:-

(a) To apprroach the owner and ask him to ----
follow the example of his Mother and dedicate the
road to the public. I have reason to believe he would
do this if the road were metalled and kept in order
by the Government and possibly named after him or

(b) To acquire the land under the Land Acquisition Decree in which case I should imagine the ---
compensation would be almost nominal as it could not
be used either for building or agricultural purposes.

B.H.Wiggins

28/10/27.

Hon C.S.

10

For your information. I
am in disagreement with Mr
Wiggins.   AMG

H. THARIA TOPAN

55 SHANGANI

Zanzibar 14th November 1928

U R G E N T.

25

The Director,

Public Work Department,

ZANZIBER.

Sir,

I am informed that you have stored some pipes on my property at Bufwacha and at Msufini. I am further informed that you intend to pass a pipe through my ~~property~~ private road, Fareji Maringo.

I shall therefore thank you to let me know if my information is correct. If the answer is affirmative then I would request you to pointout to me under what power you are authorised to use, and pass a pipe through, a private property without taking permission of the owner.

Please treat this as urgent and favour me with an early reply.

I have the honour to be

Sir,

Your most obedient servant

THE EMPIRE AT WAR

BEING

A History of Imperial Co-operation up to and including the Great War

THE ROYAL COLONIAL INSTITUTE has made arrangements with the Oxford University

3. A more important enlargement of our enquiry is connected with the question of the restriction of immigration. We have sought to avoid any close consideration either of the principles underlying immigration restriction legislation or the details of their application, but we feel that there is a necessary correspondence between the rules which govern letting people into a place and those which govern turning them out, and that it is impossible to determine the latter without bearing the former to some extent in mind. So far as the United Kingdom is concerned, the position at present is that no British subject can be refused admission and no British subject can be deported. British protected persons are aliens in the United Kingdom, and do not enjoy all the privileges attaching to British nationality. We recognize that it would not be reasonable to expect all the Colonies and Protectorates to follow the United Kingdom in according free admission to all persons who are British subjects and refraining from deporting any such persons. Conditions of climate and

Warning To Zanzibar Europeans

Re-Export Cloves Hitherto Imported By Mistake, Says Representative Of Zanzibar Association

Dr. Biharilal Anantani, Bar-at-Law, the Editor of the "Zanzibar Voice" and the representative in India of the Indian National Association in Zanzibar, issue the following statement to the Press:——

As a representative in India of the Indian National Association in Zanzibar, I am informed that undeterred by the successful boycott of cloves in India under the auspices of the Indian National Congress, in order to give India a fight in this direction a European firm has shipped certain quantity of cloves for Madras and Calcutta again and this time also to Marmagoa, a Portuguese port, with a view to a smuggle them into India. I congratulate the Congress Boycott Committee in Bombay on its prompt action issuing instructions to Belgaum and Londa Congress Committees on the Indo-Portuguese Frontier to place the Congress cordon on the entry of the unwanted cloves into India. I am confident what not a grain of cloves would enter India through such routes.

Let Them Understand

The incident however, is not without its significance. It in effect demonstrates the determination of the opposition to give India a defeat in her righteous and hitherto an eye-opening struggle to vindicate her national honour abroad. The leniency shown by the Congress Boycott Committee in Bombay in allowing the defaulters to re-export the quantity hitherto imported to European ports in the past is being abused. I therefore venture to press for re-exportation of such quantities from Bombay, Madras and Calcutta to Zanzibar Let those in Zanzibar supporting the suicidal and fantastic monopoly of the Clove Growers' Association designed to oust Indians from the trade of the country of their domicile thus have the practical demonstration of India's strength to retaliate against any sinful measures.

This and this alone is likely to open the eyes of the enemies of India and satisfy our countrymen in Zanzibar suffering under a grievous wrong to them.

Another point that occurs to me for appeal to the European firms in India acting as agents of the Commercial firms, banks and shipping lines is that in view of their business relationship in India with Indian business men, depositors and shippers, it is indeed upto them to instruct their principals in Zanzibar, in time, not to have anything to do with cloves in any form or shape so long as justice is not done to India in this respect.

Successful Boycott.

The unofficial measure of boycott has been wonderfully successful. The official measures of introduction of provincial embargo first and central next is under consideration and to avoid bitterness is entirely left to those who soil their hands with cloves under the present conditions of trade.

We are on the threshold of victory. Let down by our own Government and by a section in the Central Legislature we have demonstrated to the world our strength by means of boycott. Every word of appeal, warning and remonstrance we addressed to the Zanzibar Government and the Colonial Office has been proved to be true by action.

No monopoly in the world could ever be maintained indefinitely by any amount of an overdrafts by Banks even when guaranteed by Governments, howsoever mighty, without an outturn of business. The deadlock, painful as it is to us, has sufficiently told itself on the originators of the crime and it is for India now to see that victory is finally achieved through the means which I have ventured to suggest above and thereby to add a glorious chapter to the history of her national uplift.

Britain's Game in East Africa.

—:o:—

(*The Negro World, New York.*)

—:o:—

British statesmen are always looking ahead in order to safeguard the interests of their nation, always at the expense of some body. It is a well known fact that they quickly got reconciled to the loss of their thirteen American colonies at the end of the eighteenth century because they envisaged greater glory in the conquest of India and plunder of her fabulous wealth. Now that the time has come to lose in fact, if not in name also, that "brightest jewel" of the British Empire, they are already looking around to see where they can carry on their game of preying on some one else.

Luckily for the British things have shaped rather well for them in East Africa. They have Uganda and Kenya as their crown colonies, they have a mandate over Tanganyika and they have a virtual protectorate over Zanzibar, the island of cloves. The British imperialists have been dreaming of building out of these territories an East African Empire for, Britain to replace the -to-be-shortly lost Indian Empire. In the very near future things will come to a head and Great Britain will seriously bid for the annexation of the mandated territory of Tanganyika, without, which that East African Empire will not be a reality. What with the Japanese successful defiance of the weak-kneed League of Nations, Britain will have a fair chance of consolidating her imperialistic schemes. She will be in a position to eliminate Italian and French objections and possibly German also, by disintegrating the Portuguese Empire in Africa, which will be parcelled out among arch imperialists of Europe.

But such adjustment which might be profitable momentarily will but start a serious struggle for the ultimate emancipation of Africa from these European imperialists This is, therefore an excellent opportunity for the forces of the Universal Negro Improvement Association to reorganize on a more solid basis and carry on the struggle right on the soil of Africa to prepare for the ultimate redemption of the Fatherland. As we have repeatedly said, there shall be no world-peace or social readjustment as long as Africa remains under the heels of imperialist tyranny.

Let us get ready.

I beg to bring to your notice

est to myself as involving my

ily.

As I am myself a foreigner,

England and married to a cou

ve taken the advice of one o

lish experts in international

is opinion for your considera

I am at your disposal to cal

R.

ntial.

Downing Street,

18 December, 1922.

Sir,

I have the honour to acknowledge the receipt of your Confidential despatch of the 3rd of November, and to inform you that I approve the grant of an annuity of £100 to Frau Emily Ruete, daughter of the late Seyyid-Said, Sultan of Muscat, as from the 1st of January 1923, on the conditions laid down in paragraph 7 of your despatch.

2.　I have asked the Secretary of State for Foreign Affairs to arrange for the issue of this annuity in Germany at the rate of exchange current from time to time.　The Crown Agents for the Colonies will refund the payments on behalf of the Government of Zanzibar to the Vote for Diplomatic and Consular Services.

I have the honour to be

Sir,

Your most obedient
humble servant,

Devonshire.

BRITISH RESIDENT
AT ZANZIBAR.

10 JAN 1923

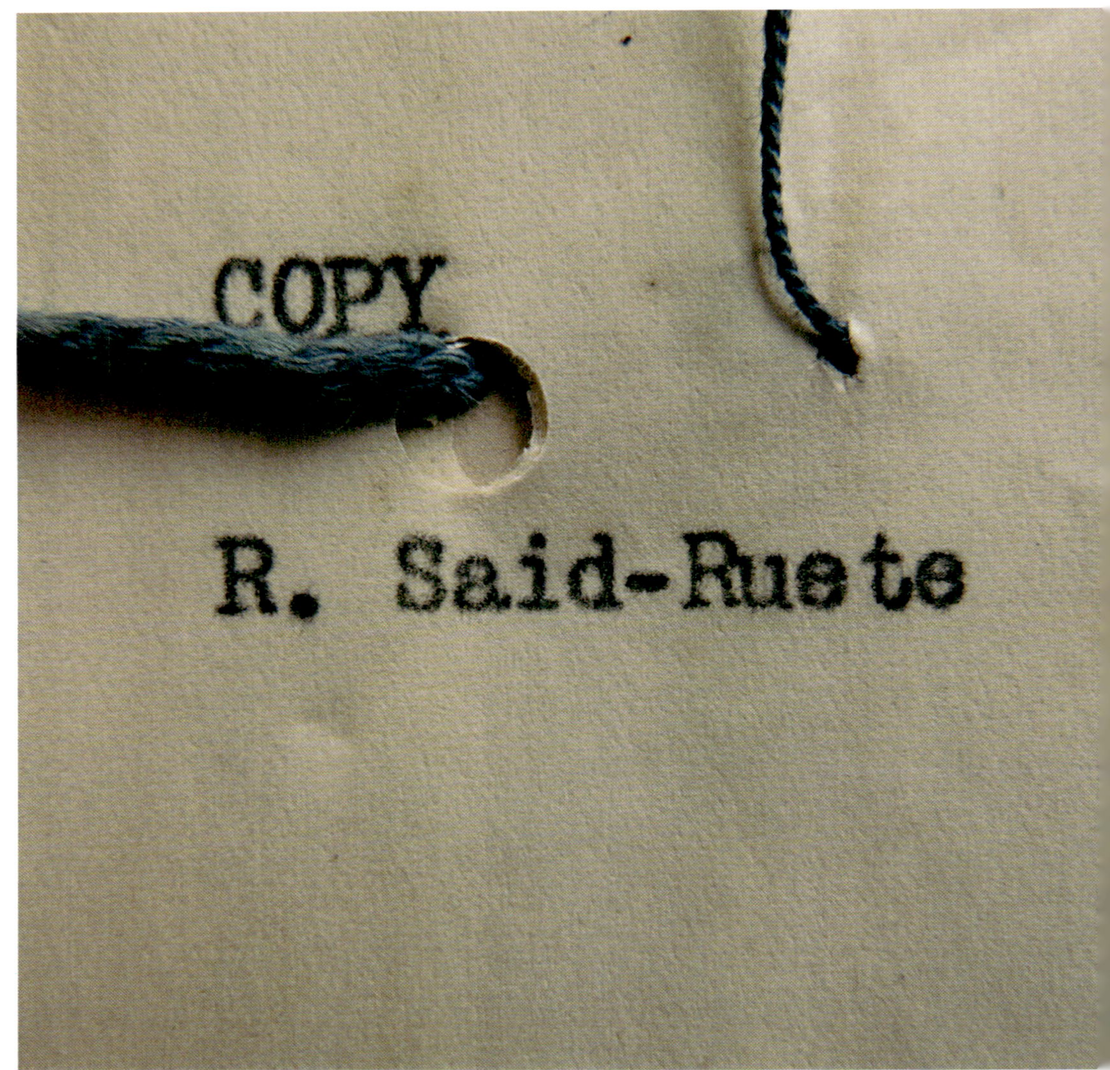
COPY
R. Said-Ruete

KHALIFA BIN HARUB

SULTAN OF ZANZIBAR

KHALIFA BIN HARUB SULTAN OF ZANZIBAR - ZANZIBAR

I THANK YOU MOST WARMLY FOR YOUR KIND TELEGRAM OF
GREETING STOP I AM DELIGHTED TO BE IN MOMBASA WITH
ITS HISTORIC ASSOCIATIONS WITH THE ARAB PEOPLE AND
MORE PARTICULARLY WITH YOUR FAMILY

ELIZABETH R

SUBJECT.

Floggings 1914
Professor Simpson's report
Distressed British Subjects Erasmus

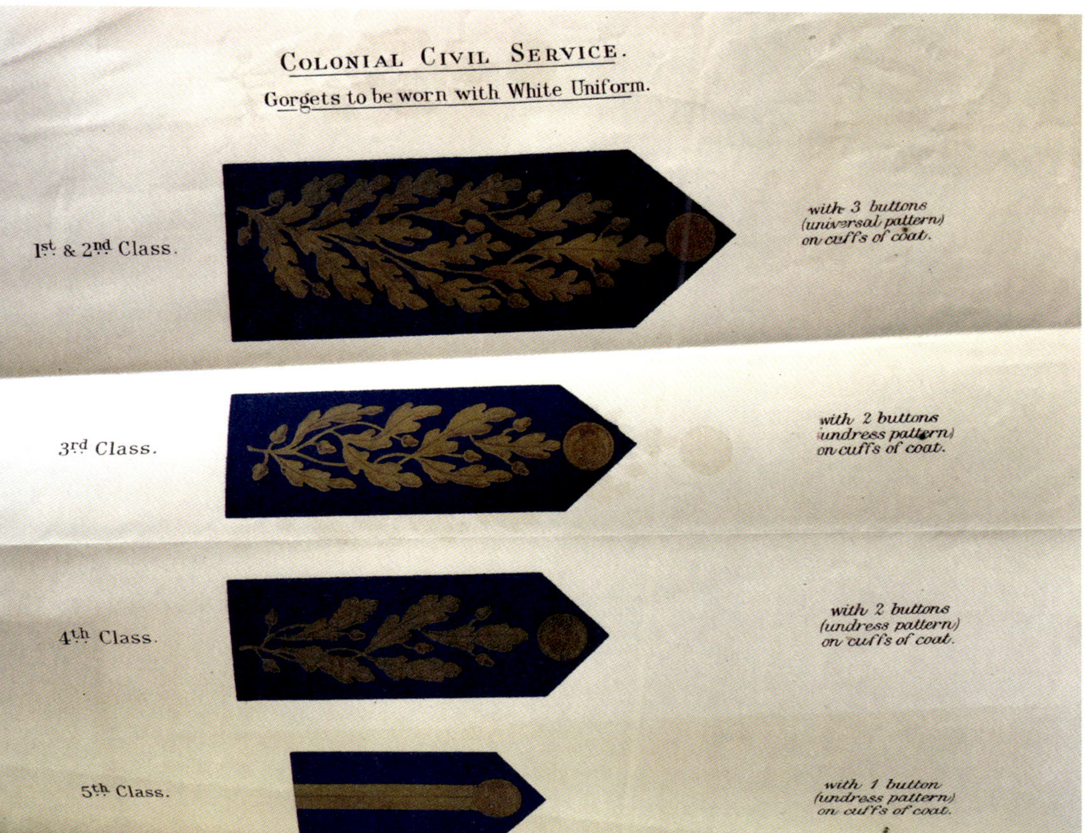
COLONIAL CIVIL SERVICE.
Gorgets to be worn with White Uniform.
1st & 2nd Class.
with 3 buttons
(universal pattern)
on cuffs of coat.
3rd Class.
with 2 buttons
(undress pattern)
on cuffs of coat.
4th Class.
with 2 buttons
(undress pattern)
on cuffs of coat.
5th Class.
with 1 button
(undress pattern)
on cuffs of coat.

2.

agreements, but if they remain after that my responsibility for their return ceases.   Perhaps some arrangement
might be come to whereby on a recommendation by the Railway Magistrate that any coolie is without visible means
of subsistence or is a bad character you might exercise
your powers of deportation, but at present the Railway
is powerless in the matter.

                       I have the honor to be,

                           Sir,

                       Your obedient servant,

                         MANAGER & CHIEF ENGINEER,

                            Uganda Railway.

                                        NAIROBI,
                                        17th August, 1946.

Your Excellency,

        I trust Your Excellency will forgive me for
intruding upon your most valuable time once again on the subject
of admission of Ismaili students in Dental and Medical Colleges
and Universities in Great Britain. But the matter is so vital
to the welfare of my people in East Africa that I feel I cannot
leave the country without appealing to Your Excellency once
again to assist my followers in this matter.

        The Academical Year begins in October and there are
half a dozen Ismaili students waiting to proceed to England
if they can get admission.   Three wish to go in for Dentistry
and the other three for Medicine.   If they do not get
admission at once they will lose one whole year they can ill
afford to waste.   One of these students is a girl, who is
proceeding for Dentistry, under a scholarship from me.

        I dealt with the serious position of dental
facilities for my people in this country in my speech at the
Weighing Ceremony, but I would reiterate that not one in
thousands of my followers are able to get any dental treatment
in their life and the havoc played by this lack of attention
to their teeth is appalling and has to be seen to be believed.
I am not exaggerating when I say that the health and even the
very existence of the future generation of my people will be
jeopardized unless this serious position is immediately remedied.

        I was gratified to have an assurance from Your
Excellency that you will come to the rescue of my people and
I am appealing to Your Excellency to graciously expedite this
matter and assist these students to get an admission in various
colleges from October 1946 and for a minimum of six students
in Dentistry for October 1947.

                                Yours very sincerely,

                                (Sgd.)   Aga Khan

EXCELLENCY THE GOVERNOR OF TANGANYIKA,
        GOVERNMENT HOUSE,
            DAR ES SALAAM.

15c., black   2018
Embroidered text in black silk on cotton
63.5 × 93 × 1 cm

CONGO FREE STATE.

LIST OF TREATIES WITH FOREIGN POWERS, &c.

Austria - Hun- gary	24th Dec., 1884.	Declarations. Recognition of Asso- ciation, Trade, &c. . . . .
,, ..	26th Feb., 1885.	" Berlin Act." See Africa (General).

$\frac{1}{2}$ **d., white**   2018
Embroidered cotton appliqué, edged in silk thread
166 × 146 × 1.2 cm

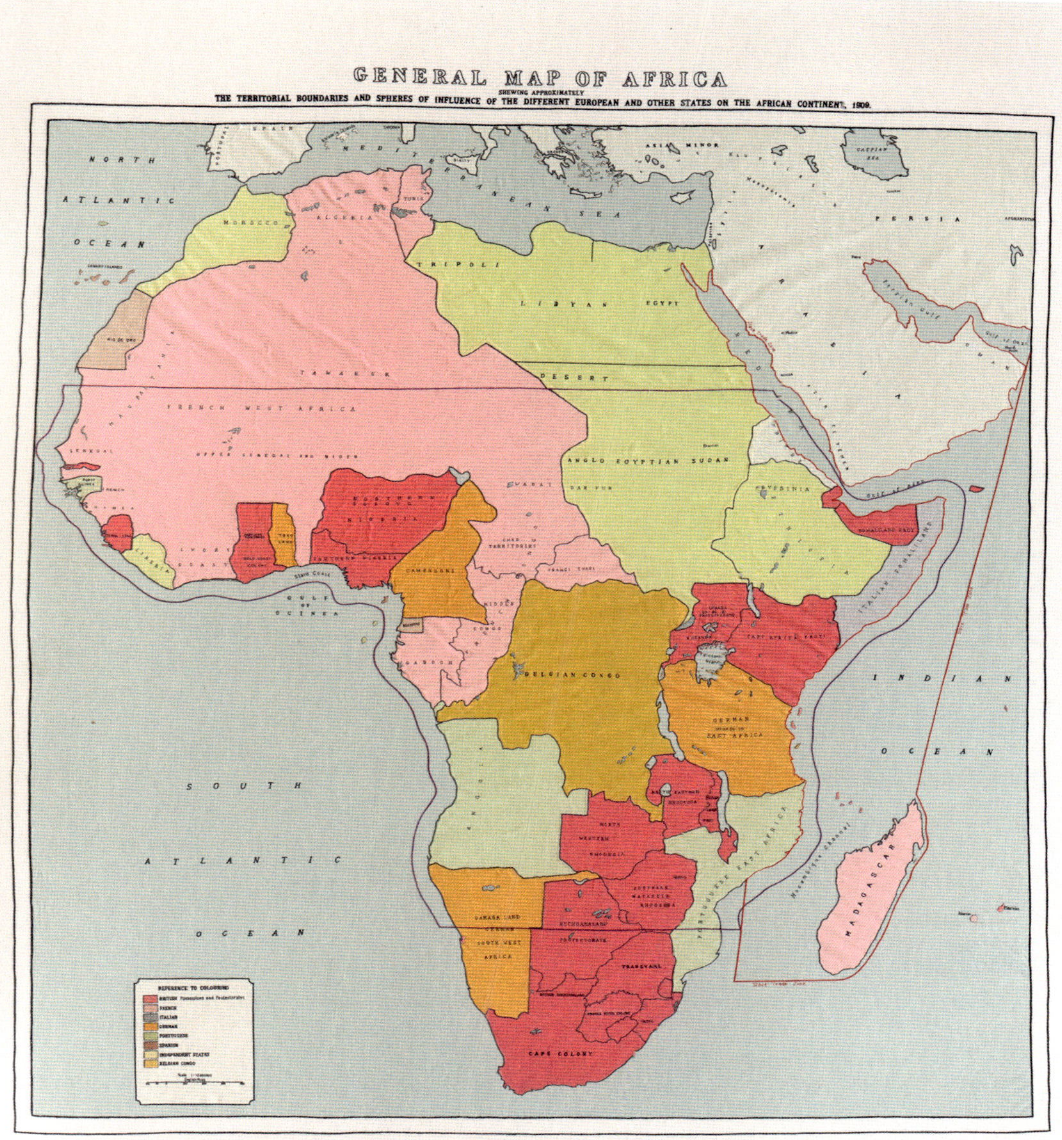

GENERAL MAP OF AFRICA
SHEWING APPROXIMATELY
THE TERRITORIAL BOUNDARIES AND SPHERES OF INFLUENCE OF THE DIFFERENT EUROPEAN AND OTHER STATES ON THE AFRICAN CONTINENT, 1909.
NORTH ATLANTIC OCEAN
MEDITERRANEAN SEA
ASIA MINOR
PERSIA
SPAIN
MOROCCO
ALGERIA
TUNIS
TRIPOLI
LIBYAN
EGYPT
DESERT
SAHARA
FRENCH WEST AFRICA
UPPER SENEGAL AND NIGER
SENEGAL
ANGLO EGYPTIAN SUDAN
DAR FUR
ABYSSINIA
SOMALILAND
ITALIAN SOMALILAND
NORTHERN NIGERIA
SOUTHERN NIGERIA
IVORY COAST
GOLD COAST
TOGO LAND
SIERRA LEONE
LIBERIA
GULF OF GUINEA
CAMEROONS
LAKE TERRITORY
FRENCH CONGO
GABOON
CONGO
BELGIAN CONGO
EAST AFRICA
GERMAN EAST AFRICA
INDIAN OCEAN
SOUTH ATLANTIC OCEAN
RHODESIA
NORTH WESTERN RHODESIA
PORTUGUESE EAST AFRICA
MADAGASCAR
DAMARA LAND
GERMAN SOUTH WEST AFRICA
BECHUANALAND PROTECTORATE
TRANSVAAL
ORANGE RIVER COLONY
CAPE COLONY
REFERENCE TO COLOURING
BRITISH Possessions and Protectorates
FRENCH
ITALIAN
GERMAN
PORTUGUESE
SPANISH
INDEPENDENT STATES
BELGIAN CONGO

Lead White
Zarina Bhimji

Thank you

Andrew Love, Achim Borchardt-Hume, Abdullah Hussein, Professor Abdul Sheriff, HE Abeid Amani Karume, Alex Farquharson, Alice Murrell, Allison Deutsch, Beit al-Ajaib – The House of Wonders Zanzibar and staff, Dr Amina Amier, Ann Gallagher, Anna Mandlik, Artsadmin staff, Carolyn Kerr, Cecilia Wee, Duro Olowu, Fatma Allo, Gabriella Nugent, Gavin Brabant, Grieger & staff, Gill Lloyd, Hand & Lock, Hannah Pierce, all at HENI Publishing, Herman Lelie, Sheikha Hoor Al Qasimi, Jacky Klein, Jessica Jane Pile, Joe Hage, Jeremy Lewison, Judith Knight, Kasia Kolendarska, Kate Bush, Lang GmbH, Lauren Mele, Manick Govinda, Mat Price, Mikei Hall, Dr. Manu Chandaria, Mahmmoud Al Sheikh, Martin Lesanto-Smith, National Library of Scotland, National Museum of African Art Smithsonian Institution, Professor Neelika Jayawardane, Neil Juggins, Mr Othman Khamis Hassan Hamad Hassan, Paul Chaulo, Phoebe Adler, Pro Centre, Reem Shadd, Renny Lee, Remi Onabanjo, Robin Smith, Mr Salum S. Salum, Sandhini Poddar, Sharjah Art Foundation and staff, Shiraz & Gulzar D Alibhai, Dr Simon Groom, Sofia Karamani, Stefan Reuter, Stefania Bonelli, The Zanzibar National Archives and staff, Zanzibar Serena Hotel and Zoe Whitley.

Produced by Zarina Bhimji Studio and assisted by Artsadmin

Lead White has been commissioned by Sharjah Art Foundation

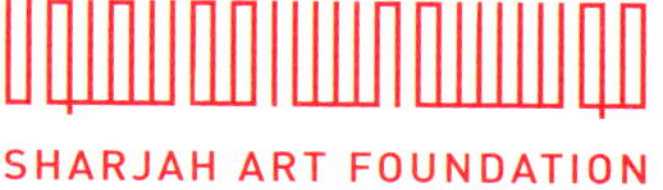

SHARJAH ART FOUNDATION

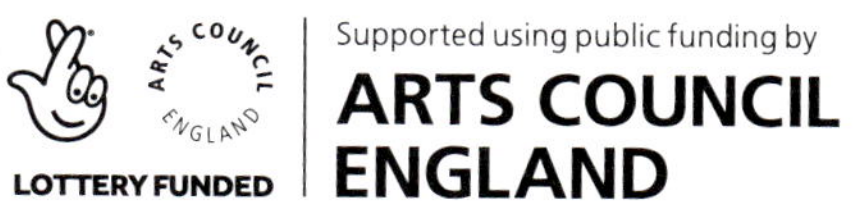

Zarina Bhimji Studio

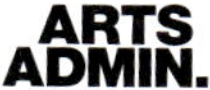

Published on the occasion of Tate Britain's 'Spotlight' display of Zarina Bhimji's *Lead White*
19 November 2018 – 2 June 2019

Lead White, 2018
Installation of 111 C-prints mounted on paper, dimensions variable

ISBN 978-1-9121221-8-9

Designed by Herman Lelie and Zarina Bhimji
Layout by Stefania Bonelli
Copyedited by Phoebe Adler and Matt Price
Printed in Italy by Editoriale Bortolazzi Stei
Photographic reproduction by Grieger GmBH, Dusseldorf

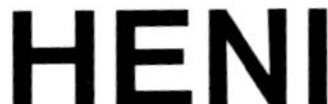 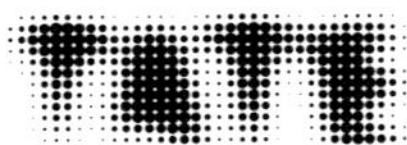